Unlock the Vault

A Blueprint For Building Wealth With Fractional Ownership

Weather Market Storms and Enjoy Long-Term
Security With An Emerging New Asset Class

Michael Fox-Rabinovitz

ISBN: 978-1-7358994-4-2 (Paperback)
ISBN: 978-1-7358994-3-5 (Ebook)

Printed in New York, United States.

Contents

Preface

This book was initially conceived as a companion book to "Own a Fraction, Earn a Fortune." Many readers fell in love with the concept of fractional investing. They embraced it as a part of their investment strategy, wanted to explore a broader range of possibilities on the spectrum. During my research, it became clear that this volume would not be simply a complement to the original manuscript but a valuable standalone work highlighting an investment strategy that is distinct and powerful on its own. Those already familiar with the topic will learn about multiple new and unusual opportunities, indulge their curiosity, and increase their understanding of various aspects of the fractional investment space. Those who are just now dipping their toes into the fractional pond for the first time and have not yet read "Own a Fraction, Earn a Fortune" will be starting their journey from a slightly different perspective. Still, they will likely be inspired to explore this world in more detail after finishing reading it.

The first half of this book showcases a variety of fractional revenue opportunities, as opposed to a fractional ownership model for collectibles. It provides a different insight into the partial ownership investment strategy, emphasizing profit not from capital appreciation but rather from income derived from participating in various cash flow streams or transactions.

The second half of the book covers some of the collectible asset classes not covered in "Own a Fraction, Earn a Fortune," as they are slightly more obscure and, while retaining high-profit potential, lack the magnitude of upside potential relative to the more mainstream asset classes that were included. Nonetheless, it is important to be aware of as many potential pockets of value as possible to understand the full range of options available in the market. Some of the items described may well make their way into future opportunity portfolios.

Investing in fractional revenue opportunities requires adopting a slightly different mindset from the one employed in investing in fractional assets. The core skill set required here is the ability to understand the business models, profit drivers and risk factors involved. You will, in effect, take an approach similar to one that venture capital firms would employ when investing in startups. This is a more nuanced and advanced set of opportunities, requiring even more dedication and investment savvy than the collectible investment space. Unlike collectible assets, these investments are structured to provide ongoing positive cash flow for medium to long timeframes. This investment strategy does not rely on capital appreciation and exits via a sale of the underlying asset to generate profit. In effect, you are continuously de-risking the investment via an ongoing return of capital. Or, if you prefer to think of it another way, you may choose to invest the profits as a way to more seamlessly employ a reinvestment strategy that will allow the magic of compounding to take place. Exploring this in conjunction with the core collectible approach creates a remarkable investment portfolio. It will combine inflation protection and capital appreciation features of collectibles with ongoing cash flows from fractional revenue opportunities. This is indeed the "Holy Grail" of balanced investment portfolios. I am excited to show you these additional ways to cement your financial well-being and help you continue on the path to creating financial security and building sustainable wealth.

Before we embark upon the quest to learn about this asset class, you need to have a clear expectation of what you will get from this book.

You WILL learn:

- some of the main niche businesses accessible via a fractional revenue framework
- the key value drivers to consider when evaluating opportunities in specific niches
- how to use an analytical framework to make an informed decision about which assets to include in your portfolio

You will NOT learn:

- rigorous quantitative analysis of diversification benefits to the portfolio from incorporating collectibles and niche business revenue streams
- tools to perform in-depth financial analysis of fractional revenue opportunities
- opinions on asset classes future prices or values
- specific investment, tax, or wealth management advice

FRACTIONAL REVENUE SHARES

The first half of the book will describe the concepts, mechanics and valuation metrics for some of the most well-known and popular frameworks that allow fractional participation in a revenue stream or profit upside from a range of business models built around investing in or financing of very recognizable assets or activities. The definition of "fractional" investment is a lot less clear-cut in this world than in the fractional collectible platform paradigm. It encompasses a gamut of ways to take part in these unique and exciting wealth-generating opportunities. Let us now venture into this territory that is uncharted for most and open our minds to the possibilities.

ALCOHOL

Whisky Cask Investments

Scotch whisky begins life as cereals allowed to begin germination with yeast added to ferment the mixture. The fermentation result, which is basically beer, is distilled to produce a clear-colored, sharp distillate that is not suitable for drinking and is stored for maturation in naturally permeable, second-hand oak barrels at an alcohol content of about 60%. The barrels, which will previously have stored bourbon, sherry or port, offer a richly complex semi-permeable membrane through which gases can pass. The chemistry of the distillate changes subtly as it reacts with the second-hand wood and the air. They work their way through the barrel wall in both directions, slowly weakening the alcoholic strength of the fluid for a regulated minimum of 3 years (before that, it cannot be called whisky and is designated as "new-make spirit") and all the way to 18 years and beyond. During maturation, the drink continually improves, becoming more valuable to the brand owners as it does so. The mature product, which we know as whisky, comes out of a cask at slightly over 50% alcohol (cask strength) and is diluted to about 40% for bottling and sale.

The improvement due to maturation is the primary economic reason behind investing in the whisky maturing process, generating returns for an exclusive community for hundreds of years. The cask's appeal over bottled whiskey is that whisky continues to age in the cask, whereas this process stops once it has been bottled. The easiest and best path to realize value is simply selling the cask off once it's reached maturity. Let someone else take on the risk and hassle of bottling the spirit and selling it as a labeled product. The main exit strategies are (1) selling the casks directly to whisky brands in need of mature stock, (2) to private investors or collectors, who often wish to bypass large portions of the maturation period by purchasing mature stock or, (3) at a whisky auction. Those investors who can hold on to their casks for longer than the bare minimum of three to five years will reap the biggest benefits. The demand for whisky matured for eight or more years is generally more significant and can provide a much higher investment return. To make the final product even more appealing and valuable, it is possible to finish the product in a different cask after the initial maturing period to create a unique taste profile.

Should the investor decide to take delivery and do his own bottling, there are many extra costs once the whisky is matured and deemed ready for bottling. The initial purchase price normally covers only the cask and spirit up until it's deemed ready to bottle. In Scotch's case, the whisky must be bottled in Scotland, a process that includes bottling, printing and labeling costs. After that, there are duties, excise, taxes, import costs, customs fees, shipping costs, additional costs of obtaining a liquor license for importing a commercial quantity of alcohol and securing storage space for the 300+ bottles. Casks are stored in a bonded warehouse, regularly checked by whisky experts and fully insured for ten years against fire, theft, accidental damage and spoilage.

Purchasing cask whisky is often compared to investing in en primeur wine (discussed in the next section), although the two are, in fact, very different. With wine, the specific year matters, as the grapes need to have the right amount of sun and rain at the right time. With whisky, while the quality of barley, malt and water along with the wood the whisky matures in play a crucial part in deciding the quality of the final outcome, the main determinant of value is maturity. However, a cask investor needs to be very diligent about making sure that the product is stored correctly to avoid unpleasant surprises once it comes time to sell. While many people assume that as long as their whisky is stored in a cask in a bonded warehouse, no harm can come to it, there is a finite time in which to sell a cask. If a 50-year-old cask drops below the legal minimum of 40% alcohol, it will be subsequently deemed worthless, effectively wasting half a century of work and wait. Casks can also leak and become overly woody. Cask owners should ensure that their casks are checked, regauged (measured as to the quantity of liquid in the cask and percentage of alcohol content) and sampled annually. Once a bottle is sealed with a cork, it's a finished product, but with a cask, it's a moving target: it needs to be checked, sampled and looked after by a safe set of hands.

There is a genuine commercial demand at the end of maturation, which drives excellent exit prices. The initial cost for investors covers the cask, roughly 200 liters of spirit inside the cask (casks are made by hand and are not all exactly 200 liters), plus the storage and insurance for ten years. Typically, each cask will yield between 350 and 420 standard 70cl bottles, depending on how long whisky is aged. The whisky's title and ownership are registered in the investor's name, and as the owner of the asset, the investor can sell (or bottle) the whisky at any time. The cash price for 8-year-old Scotch whisky bought new and sold each year between 2010-2019 shows average historical returns of 15.4% per annum. Storage fees brought the annual return down to 11.7%. The ultimate objective is to make money, which means divorcing yourself from the romance and fun of the affair and focusing purely on ensuring every last drop of spirit is sold at a profit.

Where to get a cask:

https://www.whiskyinvestdirect.com/

https://whiskeywealthclub.com/

https://www.cask88.com/

https://www.rarewhisky101.com/barrel-brokerage

Value Metrics: Maturation time, Stock condition, Input quality, Distiller skill, Brand

Maturation time: The longer whisky is allowed to mature, the more valuable it becomes. This is due to two main factors: (1) the quality improves the longer it interacts with the wood and (2) a lesser supply of high maturity product due to portions of stock bottled at lower maturities. The latter makes the remaining whisky that much scarcer and more valuable.

Stock condition: Multiple issues can affect the stock's value and quantity while it is still in the barrel. Alcohol content can drop below the legal minimum of 40%, casks can leak, and too much wood can enter the flavor making the product undrinkable. Regular checks and inspections of the barrel and the liquid inside are vital. Regardless of maturity, stock in poor condition is going to be worthless.

Input quality: Ensuring that all the key ingredients, such as barley, malt and water, are of top grade is imperative in getting a high-quality product upon maturation. Part of the distiller's skill is locating the key inputs and making sure they are supplied in the right quantity and correct sequence. There are very few ingredients, and unwavering attention to detail from the very beginning makes all the difference between a top-quality product and the rest. Care must also be taken throughout the distillation process to maintain the highest hygiene and food safety levels.

Distiller skill: A master distiller will be responsible for supervising and training staff to perform specific tasks, including milling, mashing, fermenting and, of course, distilling. During distillation, the liquid is heated to a vapor that is then pushed along to the condenser, where it is cooled back into a liquid. The resulting distillate is more concentrated in ethanol and certain flavor compounds than the liquid it left behind in the still. The first compounds released in the still as it heats up are the lower boiling point compounds we call "heads" that include methanol, acetaldehyde and lighter esters. Once the distiller makes the first cut, the heads are generally either disposed of or redistilled to collect more alcohol from them. After the distiller has decided that the incoming distillate's quality is good enough to keep for drinking purposes, they will cut to "hearts" or what will ultimately become the finished product. They contain the bulk of the ethanol required, along with flavors and aromas that make each spirit unique. When the emerging hearts distillate starts to take on unpleasant aromas and flavors, the distiller will make another cut and divert the distillate flow to another container for the remainder of the distillation run. The distillate at this point is called "tails," and just like the heads, tails will either be disposed of or (most often) redistilled to collect more alcohol. The number of heads and tails allowed to bleed into the heart is one of the ways a distiller makes his mark and decides the distillery's house character.

Brand: Reputation of a particular distillery can add a great deal of value to the final product. A good one will have a demonstrable track record of successfully going through the entire process from start to finish multiple times. Having prior matured products highly reviewed sets a good benchmark, as well as a reasonable expectation for future batches, and thus figures into the expected quality and value of the matured product.

En Primeur Wines

"En primeur" or the wine futures market refers to the opportunity to invest in wine while it is still in barrels. Purchasing "en primeur" allows investors to secure wines that may have very limited quantities and be difficult to buy after they are released. The wines most commonly offered en primeur are from Bordeaux, Burgundy, the Rhône Valley and Port, although other regions are adopting the practice. It's a risky business as the vintage could end up with poor marks from critics, but when the wine turns out well, there's a chance for a healthy 20-40% increase in value after only one or two years.

For Bordeaux, it all begins in late March or early April, when châteaus host tastings for the trade to evaluate the potential quality of the vintage harvested during the previous autumn. These wines have just gone into the barrel and are still about two years from reaching the market in bottles. The châteaux then release for sale a 'tranche' or proportion of their total production in strict allocation to intermediaries known as courtiers. They take a small percentage, and the right to sell the futures is then passed on to the main wine brokers, known as négociants, who sell the en primeur offers to wine merchants and importers. The wines are released in several tranches, and then prices are adjusted up or down according to the previous tranche's success. The first tranche is usually only sold to people who bought in previous years or will commit to buying bad vintages too. The second tranche will almost always be at a higher price. If the négociants don't buy what they are offered (in a bad year), they risk forfeiting their allocation for the next year (which may be a great year). This system dates back to the 18th century when Bordeaux merchants visited the local or regional chateaux before harvest. The modern-day en primeur system was institutionalized in the 1970s with the advent of Bordeaux en primeur tasting week.

Payment is made at an early stage, 12 or 18 months prior to the official release of a vintage, and the balance (tax and duty) when they are finally released, with a typical lot being a case of 6 or 12 75cl bottles. Thus, a stake in the wine is purchased before the commodity has become a finished product, basically acting like a futures market for wine. In the period between purchase and delivery, the price of the wine is likely to change, giving this market a certain speculative character. Once bottled wines are shipped by the chateau to bonded warehouses in the buyer's country, he has the option of taking delivery or letting the merchant sell the bottles on his behalf. Key benefits of "en primeur" purchases are getting superior brands at the lowest price with the maximum period for maturity and potential growth in value, security of provenance from wines delivered via the most direct route from the Château, and easily liquidated stock after physical delivery.

While a completely reliable mechanism for identifying what to buy does not exist, there are five things that good en primeur investments have in common.

1. Well-backed by a range of critics at the initial tasting.

2. Backed again by the critics once re-tasted in bottle, a high-scoring wine en primeur will need to have its score confirmed once the wine is bottled.

One-off high scoring wines en primeur tend to peak in price just before they are re-tasted.

3. Wines from up-and-coming properties on an upward curve in terms of the critical evaluations whose release prices still have yet to catch up with their new-found status are more likely to be underpriced relative to their value and represent a better investment.

4. There is a compelling story to tell about the property's upward quality trajectory, be it a change in ownership, winemaker, or style.

5. Scarce wines for which one needs an allocation. There are many wines theoretically offered en primeur that are practically impossible to buy without a history of buying them. Some of these are long-standing (such as Petrus, Le Pin and Lafleur in Pomerol), but numerous new cuvees from tiny properties spare no expense to make the best wine possible have similar characteristics.

Where to get a barrel:

https://www.wineinvestment.com/

https://www.vinovest.co/

Value metrics: Brand, Critic reviews, Vintage, Geography

Brand: If the wine is produced by a famous brand with limited availability, it will be very scarce and hard to obtain and thus quite valuable. The best deals can be had from up-and-coming producers whose brand is known and looked upon favorably, but is not yet fully established as a household name. Positive changes in brand development, such as a new winemaker, owner, or process improvement, will also affect the brand's perception and strength, and thus the price.

Critic reviews: It is important that the reviews are favorable and are consistent or trending up from initial tasting from the barrels to re-testing once the wine is in the bottle. As this is the only somewhat objective metric, when taking the reviews from key critics in aggregate, its value will strongly depend on this.

Vintage: As with all wines, getting a superior vintage when the weather, elements and terroir come together to create a perfect combination is the key to success. If such conditions happen to exist for a particular vintage as it is being put into barrels, it is likely that once matured, this wine will be in very high demand.

Geography: Traditionally, only flagship French wines have been offered en primeur along with port, but other geographies are adopting and embracing the practice as well. While the iconic French terroirs still dominate the market and command premium prices, other areas such as Napa Valley, Tuscany, Australia and New Zealand are adopting this practice.

WEB ASSETS

Domains

In 1848, the gold found in California sparked the Gold Rush, bringing thousands of dreamers and entrepreneurs into the wilderness to chase elusive success and big dreams. In the 1990s, another version of the Gold Rush played out in Silicon Valley. Only this time, prospectors were looking for domain names instead of nuggets of gold; easier to mine but no less rare and valuable. The common factors across both of these periods are that only the very few who were both smart and lucky actually got rich despite the hype.

Domain names are the internet equivalent of real estate. Like properties in the real world, domain names can be bought and sold for a profit, used to generate an income, or be developed and improved so that they increase in value. A domain name is simply an identification label that defines a realm of administrative autonomy, authority, or control on the Internet, based on the Domain Name System (DNS). Each element of a domain name separated by [.] is called a "label." The maximum allowed length of each label is 63 characters, and the maximum allowable length of the full domain name is 253 characters.

Domain names are used to make it easy for people to find web pages on the Internet by converting IP Addresses (numbers in the format of 11.222.33.44) into domain names (such as Google.com or MSN.com). When someone wants to visit a particular website, they do not have to remember a long string of numbers but rather just type in an easy-to-remember name. Interestingly enough, domains are never truly owned; they are simply rented from ICANN for periods of up to 10 years. ICANN (Internet Corporation for Assigned Names and Numbers) is an internationally organized, non-profit corporation that has responsibility for Internet Protocol (IP) address space allocation, protocol identifier assignment, generic (gTLD) and country code (ccTLD) Top-Level Domain name system management, and root server system management functions. These services were originally performed under a U.S. Government contract by the Internet Assigned Numbers Authority (IANA) and other entities.

One of the biggest sources of domain name inventory is expired domains. Owners must renew the domains to keep ownership of them. Every month millions of domain names expire when their owners don't pay to renew them either because they forget or simply because the potential value did not materialize. These domains then become available for anyone to register, but most decent domain names are taken the second they expire by companies using automation technology to snap them up. Investors use these so-called "dropcatching" companies like NameJet and DropCatch to acquire domains or search marketplaces like Sedo and Afternic, where millions of domain names are listed. Then they will submit offers or buy the domains at fixed prices. There are multiple ways to be an investor in the space, from "parking" the domain name for future resale, flipping it quickly, or developing it by building a website on it.

During the tech bubble, some domains initially registered by investors for $10 sold for millions. Today the prices have come down, but demand for great domain names is still strong. Every business that wants an internet site has to buy a domain name, and they all want one that is easy to remember and matches their business. Buying a domain name from a third party could cost any amount of money, but the actual ongoing required annual registration fees are still very cheap at around $7 to $10 annually. The proliferation of many domain name extensions means that it is easier than ever to choose an acceptable name if you are willing to settle for a less known extension. While at first, there were only 7 top-level domain extensions, the most popular among them being .com, .org, and .net., today, there are 1,096 top-level domains, including .book, .sports, .download, .xyz, and more.

Just as those who gambled on the Internet's potential early on received some of the choicest domain real estate, so too can those aware of new emerging trends register new domain names before the rest of the world catches on to the trend. New videogame systems, car models, trendy foods, and slang words all offer domain investors rich investment opportunities. For example, the btc.com domain sold for $1 million in 2014, but appeared utterly worthless before bitcoin came about.

There are multiple types of domains, with the three key ones being descriptive, brandable and short. Descriptive describes a product or service. Brandable can be marketed to stand for something other than the dictionary definition of the word. One-word domain names are particularly valuable, and two and three-word ones being also quite acceptable. Short domains containing just a few numbers or letters, commonly referred to as LLL for letter-letter-letter and NNNN for number-number-number-number, tend to be the most liquid.

There are many challenges to fractional domain ownership, but 2021 might be the year they are solved. By putting in place the technology, legal and tax structures required, domain investing could become a lot more liquid going forward. Such a system would allow domain owners to obtain liquidity in their assets that might not otherwise sell for a while. It will also allow investors to own a part of domain names they might otherwise not be able to afford. There have been attempts to develop this product, most recently by domain investor Aron Meystedt, who was selling shares in the domain NNR.com for $100 each. However, as of today, no comprehensive platform for fractional domain ownership exists.

Top 10 domain name sales:

1. Sex.com — $13,000,000
2. Fund.com — $9,999,950
3. Porn.com — $9,500,000
4. Porno.com — $8,888,888
5. We.com — $8,000,000

6. Diamond.com — $7,500,000
7. Z.com — $6,784,000
8. Slots.com — $5,500,000
9. Toys.com — $5,100,000
10. Clothes.com — $4,900,000

Expensive domain names not listed on the main list because they were either sold before 2003 or other assets were sold with the domains:

Insurance.com — $35,600,000
VacationRentals.com — $35,000,000
PrivateJet.com — $30,100,000
Internet.com — $18,000,000
Insure.com — $16,000,000
Hotels.com — $11,000,000
Fb.com — $8,500,000
Business.com — $7,000,000
Beer.com — $7,000,000

Value metrics: Extension, Length, Language, Geography, Stage of development, Recognition

Extension: While over 1,000 extensions exist, the classic .com still stands out as the most valuable and desired. It can be thought of as the gold standard, with other variations being secondary and thus less valuable. The ubiquitous .net and .org are the silver to .com's gold, but still stand out from the other 1,093 extensions.

Length: Short domains that contain few letters or numbers tend to be more liquid, as they are more easily recognized and easier to remember. While length is not the sole factor in determining value, discoverability and ease of memorization dramatically increase the potential number of eyeballs and the asset's price.

Language: Many countries and regions are just coming online, and thus need their own localized sites in their own languages. Knowing other languages and having the foresight to obtain valuable keywords in major markets can be a very lucrative undertaking. For example, if you don't speak Chinese, "youxi" means nothing to you, but in Chinese, "youxi" means game, and youxi.com sold for nearly $2.5 million in 2014. On a global scale, many countries around the world are just beginning to develop, especially in Asia and Africa, and this presents a unique opportunity to get in on the ground floor of the next big thing.

Geography: Domains specifically referencing geographic locations are one of the strongest ways to make money in the space, if not necessarily the fastest. A local domain like newyorksbestcoffee.com may not be worth millions, but a local business or even a franchise may happily spend thousands for it. Moreover, names related to large geographic areas and service industries, such as coloradoplumbers.com, can also be lucrative.

Stage of development: Depending on whether the domain is a name only, has a site built around it, or has been developed to include a viewer base, its value can change drastically. While an amazing domain name alone can command super-premium prices, combining it with a proven growing and monetizable user base makes it even more valuable.

Recognition: The degree of name recognition for a domain will determine its value. Ultimately, the monetization is driven by the site's name intuitiveness and discoverability. Names like hotel.com, car.com, wine.com leave little to chance and are likely to be ranked at or toward the top of any searches, thus getting maximum traffic.

Websites

A website is a collection of web pages and related content identified by a common domain name and published on at least one web server. The first website was just a page explaining the World Wide Web project. It explained how users could set up a web server to build their websites and web pages and was only accessible inside CERN and hosted on the creator's computer. It was created by a British computer scientist Sir Tim Berners-Lee working at CERN in 1990. He was knighted by Queen Elizabeth II in 2004 for his pioneering work and received the 2016 Turing Award "for inventing the World Wide Web, the first web browser, and the fundamental protocols and algorithms allowing the Web to scale." All of today's nearly 2 billion websites exist due to his amazing breakthrough.

Websites are a form of digital real estate that are designed to spin off semi-passive monthly income. They aren't static enterprises, as they need upkeep, fresh content, keyword search optimization strategies (SEO), and technical support to keep the "lights on" and the site up and running.

Types of profitable websites are blogs, content-based, and product/service sales. Blogs are informational sites that provide a regular stream of new articles. Content-based websites already have established traffic. Product/Service Sites are designed to buy or sell a product or service. Quality websites can be acquired via brokers (FEInternational.com, QuietLightBrokerage.com, AcquisitionStation.com) and marketplaces (Flippa.com, EmpireFlippers.com).

Due diligence is an essential part of evaluating the investment and involves many key points such as:

- Analyzing financial statements
- Reviewing Google Analytics and data of the website
- Studying social media to understand current reliance and potential opportunities
- Review and verification of the email list
- Verifying the website is in good standing with key advertisers
- Confirming ownership details and history of the domain name, including spam links, errors and prior bans

There are companies like https://onfolio.co that allow investors to become fractional owners of already existing and performing properties and build a portfolio of partial interests in profitable and cash-generating assets. As with other fractional investment formats, the platform takes care of asset selection, due diligence, operating costs and site management and growth in exchange for a fee.

Value metrics: Scalability, Profitability, Automation, Niche type, Revenue stability

Scalability. This indicates the site's ability to cope with an increase in demand as the user base and traffic grow, and whether that growth is sustainable. It calls for ensuring that the site design, technical specifications, hosting providers and other infrastructure components are in place to allow the site to develop and grow as fast as the internet will allow.

Profitability. This is the evaluation of current profit margins, historical trends variability, and projections. As with anything, past results do not guarantee future performance. Contributing to this are search engine rankings, which measure how frequently the site appears in the search results list when keywords are entered into search engines like Google. The number of unique visitors to a site each month is also a key contributor and a strong indicator of how visible a website has become on major search engines.

Automation. Sites that already have automation set up or provide the ability to automate tasks such as content update, user communication, advertiser management and troubleshooting with minimal additional cost are the most valuable and desirable from an efficiency perspective. The key here is evaluating the ability to leverage existing infrastructure to derive incremental value from leveraging automation to increase profitability due to this approach's cost-efficient nature.

Niche type. These opportunities have favorable future trends for growth in a specific industry, demographic or geography are best. The most desirable, but also the hardest to find niches are those that are either on the verge of exploding, or those where the investor has the experience and capacity to make them do so due to his personal brand or other factors. Websites with non-trendy niches are also of interest. They have a defensible position organically due to the limited but highly active and involved audience.

Revenue stability. This is driven by several factors such as:

- growth rate, which shows the net increase in users monthly and trend over multiple periods
- recurring revenue trends showing how many users constantly return to the site and generate revenue
- earnings volatility calculations that measure the stability of earnings over time and lack of seasonality effects and diversification of revenue from multiple sources of monetization, i.e., affiliates, direct sales, subscriptions, etc. This is the core of the business model and will be the deciding factor in site acquisition decisions.

VIRTUAL FINANCIAL ASSETS

Most people are already very familiar and comfortable with mainstream investments like real estate and bonds. Hence, the only potentially difficult part of making the leap to investing in the same asset classes in virtual worlds is the level of comfort in the stability and future potential of the gaming platform. This requires an understanding of the business model, and the ability to examine a meaningfully long track record of performance of similar undertakings.

Of games that employ RCE (Real Cash Economy) format, none come close to Entropia Universe in length of track record and demonstrated performance and data availability. When looking at blockchain-based virtual world platforms, Decentraland Metaverse is the most notable player. It utilizes an Ethereum based blockchain platform and native virtual currency to allow purchases of virtual land and real estate (as well as other NFT collectibles like art, accessories, etc.).

The examples below for each platform are meant to illustrate current category-leading projects. There is no doubt that the frameworks will be replicated and improved across a variety of worlds as RCE and blockchain-based universe spaces grow. The virtual reality market is projected to be worth $215 billion by the end of 2021, and blockchain technology is conservatively estimated to have a market size of $60 billion by 2024.

Real estate

In 2004 Ailin Graef, better known by her avatar name Anshe Chung, began amassing virtual real estate in Second Life. She started with less than $10 and became famous for becoming the first avatar to achieve a net worth of more than $1 million from business dealings conducted entirely inside a virtual world. Much of today's excitement about virtual real estate and NFT speculation can be traced back to the mythology surrounding Anshe Chung.

The reason the real estate category is positioned as separate from deeds (which can be defined as liquid tradable instruments participating in revenues from the asset) is to draw a distinction between ownership of the operating asset itself (the fractional aspect here can come in the form of a group-buy via an LLC) and ownership of securities tied to its performance.

Digital real estate has become a legitimate asset class worthy of investor consideration and one likely to appreciate exponentially over the near term. Not only is digital real estate capable of delivering outsized returns due to its alignment with the rapidly growing crypto-investment universe, but it also appears likely to become a viable store of wealth, like real-world art and real estate. Early movers in virtual real estate can get in at prices that are still affordable compared to real-world markets. Like early movers in fast-growing places in the real world, those who invest early and hold for the long term will benefit.

Entropia

The Entropia Universe is a massively multiplayer online (MMORPG) virtual universe designed by the Swedish software company MindArk based in Gothenburg. The development of the Entropia Universe (formerly Project Entropia) started in 1995 and took 7 years. On May 20, 2002, the Commercial Open Trial began. The game was made fully available to the public on January 28, 2003, with only one sci-fi-themed planet named Calypso. The backstory was that as human colonists on a distant alien planet, players from all over the world join together to develop a new civilization. Faced with robotic enemies and exotic environments, settlers hunt wild creatures, mine resources, and craft and trade items as they expand their human colony. Today Entropia Universe is estimated to have around 75,000 total players from virtually every country in the world.

A second music and pop culture-themed planet called Rocktropia was opened on April 6, 2010. The third beach-themed planet to be released was Next Island on December 8, 2010. The fourth planet launched was Arkadia, on May 25, 2011, with a theme of treasure hunting. The fifth sci-fi-themed planet was Cyrene, debuting on May 1, 2012. The sixth Arabian mythology and culture-themed planet Toulan was released on February 19, 2014. While not a planet, space is a separate area connecting all the planets that allows players to travel among planets via spaceships.

Entropia uses a micropayment business model, in which players buy in-game currency (PED - Project Entropia Dollars) with real money that can be redeemed back into U.S. dollars at a fixed exchange rate of 10:1. Thus, the game can be played to make money. Virtual items acquired within Entropia Universe have a real cash value, and just like in reality, every undertaking requires resources that cost money. A participant may, at any time, initiate a withdrawal of their accumulated PED back into U.S. dollars according to the fixed exchange rate, minus transaction fees. The minimum amount for a withdrawal is 1,000 PED ($100). One important caveat to understand is that players own nothing, as there is no legal concept of property within the game. Everything in the game, including avatars, their skills, tools, and even in-game money, are parts of the Entropia Universe system belonging to MindArk and partner companies who are licensing the use of these to the players. Security is provided by an app-based 2FA system, which provides a unique time-sensitive 6-digit code to be used together with a username and password every time you log in.

Example 1: Treasure Island

In December 2004, an island that exists only as computer bytes within an online role-playing game, Entropia Universe, was sold for $26,500 to David Storey, a 22-year-old player based in Australia, known in game as "Deathifier." Storey has complete mining and hunting taxation rights and can also allocate parcels of land to sell to other players. The $26,500 Treasure Island purchase price was made back in the first year, thanks to Storey's tireless development, salesmanship and marketing, both online and off. Storey had purchased "creature DNA" and scattered different species across the island, including rare and unique animals. This earns Storey and his investors a cool US$36,000 per annum for doing very little other than offering players the chance to kill virtual animals. Storey's income is supplemented by virtual real estate sales, both on Calypso and Planet Arkadia, another Entropia Universe destination where he is a co-owner.

Example 2: Space Resort "Club Neverdie"

In October 2005, a virtual space resort was sold for a price of $100,000. The auction began taking bids on the 21st of October, and just three days later, the buyout price was met by Jon Jacobs, known as "NEVERDIE" in game. This was the largest amount ever spent in the massive multiplayer online gaming space, surpassing the previously world record-breaking sale of the virtual Treasure Island by a factor of 4. Operating profitably from day one, the resort recouped the $100,000 in mining/hunting rights alone in its first eight months. Due to only the virtual property and the profits obtained from mining/hunting rights and property sales, the previous owner's fortune was valued at $1 million by the end of 2006. The property was listed in the Guinness World Records book in 2008 as the most valuable virtual item. In November of 2010, the asset has been broken up into smaller portions and sold off to new investors. The parcels' total purchase price was $635,000, giving its original owner a stunning ROI of 535% in just five years.

Example 3: Crystal Palace

In 2009 Erik Novak, known in game as "Buzz 'Erik' Lightyear," purchased the Crystal Palace Space Station on Planet Calypso in Entropia Universe for $330,000. In December 2018, the estate was sold to the public via an in-game share offering for $500,000. In the years he operated the property, Erik reports that he earned about $50,000 every year for a 15% annual profit on his investment. This yielded an estimated $400,000 over 8 years, more than covering his original investment. A healthy $170,000 (51% on top of the original purchase price) bonus when he sold it was the icing on the cake. The owners of the shares, i.e., the new owners of the virtual property, have enjoyed similar profits as Buzz. The shares yield about 12% annually. The price has doubled from the initial offering of $10 to around

$20 within a month of trading, making for a spectacular annualized return or providing a steady coupon for years with the capital appreciation portion to be realized upon sale.

Decentraland

The platform Decentraland stemmed from a proof-of-concept that assigned ownership of digital real estate in an infinite 2D grid initially dubbed the "Stone Age of the Decentralized." The next iteration of the project was a 3D virtual world divided into plots called the "Bronze Age," completed at the end of 2016. The Argentina-based founders, Ari Meilich and Esteban Ordano, raised $25 million in their 2017 ICO selling 40 percent of the total supply of its MANA ERC-20 token and received additional funding from several VCs such as Boost VC, Algalon Capital and Hashed. The metaverse has been open for early users and investors since 2019 and fully opened to the public in February 2020. Decentraland is still in its infancy with 20,000 users (as of this print date), but the user base is growing due to rapid development and new partnerships. The platform lets users explore and build like Minecraft and socialize like Second Life. However, Decentraland isn't like other virtual worlds because the users own it. If the Decentraland organization goes away, the world seamlessly goes on.

The latest addition to the metaverse is legendary Atari, one of the world's biggest gaming companies. Atari will be taking over a large estate of the Decentraland metaverse where gamers will be able to experience Atari's catalog of retro arcade games, including Pong, Break-Out!, Asteroids, Missile Command, and Centipede, among others. The gaming titan's recently launched Atari ERC-20 token is easily compatible with Decentraland and will also be used in the game.

Users can purchase virtual land, giving them ownership and control over the environment and applications they create within their land.

MANA, Decentraland's cryptocurrency ERC20 token, can also be used to purchase plots of LAND (in-game real estate) as well as pay for in-world goods and services. MANA itself can be bought and sold for fiat currency (USD, EUR, etc.) or other digital currencies (BTC, ETH, etc.). It is listed on exchanges such as Binance, Coinbase or Gemini, boasting a market capitalization of almost $400 million as of February 2021. This is nearly a 10-fold increase from its launch in 2017, with a single token currently trading at $0.30.

Changes to the Decentraland software are enacted through a collection of blockchain-based smart contacts. These allow participants who own MANA to vote on policy updates, land auctions and subsidies for new developments. Judging by the highly active LAND marketplace, and considering that there are Decentraland districts dedicated to gambling, music, education, adult material, shopping, gaming and many more, whose goods or services are paid for using MANA, it stands a very good chance of success. Its future price increases as its usability expands and demand for the currency grows as the supply dwindles.

LAND is a non-fungible ERC 721 token (NFT) used to define the ownership of land "parcels" representing digital real estate. This means it is unique and cannot be forged or duplicated, the same as physical land in real life. If you own and connect adjacent parcels of LAND on the map, it becomes an "Estate" and permits the owner to build higher: the more parcels you own, the higher you can build.

The Decentraland game world is split up into 90,601 units of LAND or "parcels" (43,689 private LAND parcels, 33,886 district LAND, 9,438 roads, 3,588 plazas) arranged in a 300 by 300 grid, all of which were initially sold at auction in December 2017. The address is designated with the coordinates on an X-axis, from 150 to -150, and then the coordinates on a Y-axis, from -150 to 150. Genesis, in the middle of the matrix, is at 0,0.

Roads and plazas are common spaces used for character movements and are not owned by anyone. Neighboring LAND tiles make up "Districts," which are communities built around a shared theme. District members can vote on district issues through Agora, Decentraland's voting app. All LAND prices vary drastically by location; the more valuable parcels are close to the center of the various districts (like Vegas City, Crypto Valley, or Dragon City) and near crossroads.

Today, land prices start at about 8,500 MANA for a single 16mx16m parcel (previously 10m x 10m, changed in Feb 2019), and estates currently start at about 18,000 MANA. The highest ever price paid for a LAND on the open market was 2,000,000 MANA and for an estate 2,772,000 MANA, which was an equivalent of $116,424 at the time of purchase. If that seems high, consider that in February 2021, in another blockchain game, Axie Infinity, nine extremely rare plots of land in an area called Genesis located in the center of the map and capped to 220 plots were sold for over 888 ETH or $1.5 million ($166,000 per plot). This made them the most expensive non-fungible token (NFT) sale transaction ever and left little doubt that the market for virtual real estate is just heating up. Players can rent their property out and earn yields by doing so, further increasing the land's value by hosting in-game events like concerts or art exhibits.

Such purchases are only expected to continue in the months and years ahead. As blockchain games create policies where people can choose who they wish to identify with and engage in land, property rights, governance, competition, and entertainment as they would in a real-world setting, the groundwork for complex societies emerges, complete with their own economies and systems of government.

Decentraland also offers the option to take out a mortgage on land by way of a smart contract and a unique collaboration with Ripio Credit Network. Failure to repay the mortgage within the agreed term will result in the borrower losing the paid amount and not being able to claim the LAND. No software house or entity can censor or confiscate the properties, as everything is regulated in a decentralized way on Ethereum. The purchased properties really belong to the players, who can claim their digital land at any time.

Anyone can buy, sell or rent LAND at any time, either peer-to-peer on the official Decentraland Marketplace or via the Opensea platform. The marketplace enables participants to manage and exchange LAND tokens and other in-game items such as wearables and unique names. All transactions are stored on the Ethereum blockchain as true proof of ownership. When you buy a LAND token or any other NFT, you officially, unquestionably and verifiably own it.

Value metrics: Brand, Activity volume, User price sensitivity, Cash flow stability, Track record length, Scalability, Liquidity, Platform

Brand: For a virtual property to be successful, much like in real life (IRL), the first requirement is that old customers remember it, enjoy it, trust it, and return to it regularly to use it. Equally important is that new customers can easily learn about it and want to try it for themselves. Property brand is often closely associated with the owner's (or rather his avatar's) reputation in game (more so than his activities offline), but both need to be spotless to create and sustain an atmosphere of trust and legitimacy. Building up and diligently maintaining the virtual asset's reputation is needed to ensure that current clients keep returning and attract a steady stream of new ones. Ongoing marketing campaigns, promotions, catering to customer preferences and positive recommendations from a large sample of current users are all required to establish and maintain a top brand.

Activity volume: Evaluating the number of players taking advantage of the property and spending cash there on in game activities is a key metric to understand. Hourly, daily, weekly and monthly client activity volumes and trends need to be evaluated to get comfortable with the asset's operational stability and accurately assess usage patterns. By developing and refining insights on this variable, the owners can develop and implement more tailored promotions to reduce the activity's cyclicality and increase overall revenues.

User price sensitivity: This data can only be produced for properties that have been in operation for an extended period, and where the owner was able to experiment with various pricing regimes and gather substantial data on them. A desirable outcome here is a low degree of price sensitivity, i.e.,

26

players should continue to use the service even at higher fee levels, as the service has unique or hard to substitute features, or offers a chance of outsized payoffs, and thus allows the owner more flexibility to optimize fee level so as to maximize his profit. For properties where this data is not available, it may be possible to estimate at least an acceptable range of price levels by reviewing fees charged by comparable competing properties within the same game universe.

Cash flow stability: Estimating cash flow variability, as well as levels, is crucial in getting comfortable with potential risks and future profits, i.e., the classical risk/reward analysis. This data is partially derived from activity volumes and fees, but may also include various additional revenue sources and reflect variability in operational costs and their key components. A predictable and relatively stable cash flow pattern is a very desirable feature in an existing property since it provides greater confidence in the valuation accuracy.

Track record length: This metric's importance is hard to underestimate. The risk profiles of acquiring a brand-new asset versus one with a multi-year history are drastically different. Buying a newly created asset is similar to investing in early-stage start-ups and requires a great deal of comfort with specific risks, faith in the business model, and profound subject matter expertise. On the other hand, purchasing an asset with a 5+ year documented operational record is more akin to investing in a mature firm, with smaller risks, but also likely higher upfront premiums and lower yield.

Scalability: The ability to quickly and effectively expand the range of product offerings and scale up existing ones is an excellent indicator of potential future upside that can be gained from the asset. This information may be a bit hard to obtain and requires intimate knowledge of game mechanics and familiarity with game developer speed of response, development timeframes, and ability to introduce features in a controlled manner that does not violate game balancing algorithms. However, thoroughly understanding these variables allows for a much better estimation of how potential future add-ons can increase asset value.

Liquidity: In the context of virtual assets, liquidity refers to the ease and ability to convert profits denominated in in-game currency into a range of real-world ones at a fixed rate and the time required to receive it once a withdrawal has been initiated. The ideal setup is a stable fixed conversion rate into all major currencies and a short withdrawal process, while allowing for reasonable checks against fraud and identity theft.

Platform: Financial position of the core gaming platform, its stability and degree of being up to date of its operational infrastructure, as well as the strength and skill of its development teams, need to be reviewed and evaluated carefully. Even if the property looks phenomenal by every other measure, if the core platform disappears or is unable to maintain standards and deliver new content, the entire undertaking is pointless.

Deeds

As discussed earlier, deeds are liquid tradable instruments participating in revenues from the asset. The concept of deeds has been very well developed inside Entropia Universe, with 5 deeds currently being traded on an in-game platform. These represent revenue streams from various parts of the universe. Additionally, there is an indication that individual land areas on each planet may get the ability to issue shares in the future. Below is an overview of the 2 oldest and most popular instruments: CLD (Calypso) and AUD (Arkadia Underground). The other 3 are AMD (Arkadia Moon), CPD (Crystal Palace) and AGD (Ancient Greece), representing revenues from other specific locations within the universe.

Entropia Universe: Calypso Land Deeds

On November 1, 2012, one of the most ambitious undertakings in the gaming world took place. Through an in-game auction system, Entropia Universe offered 60,000 deeds for Planet Calypso, priced at $100 each. This raised $6MM by selling 50% of Planet Calypso's gross revenue in perpetuity (effectively giving Calypso a $12MM valuation).

The revenue pool generated from gross revenue derived as a percentage of user transactions in an about $400MM a year economy on Calypso was divided evenly among all Calypso Land Deeds (CLD). This entitled the avatar of the deedholder to 1/60,000 of each weekly payout. It was a complete gamble on future tax revenues from a virtual world, but the offer was successful. The deeds sold out over a few months, with the largest investor spending a staggering $2.5 million on deeds.

Every week the shareholders received on average 35 cents, yielding an $18.2 or 18.2% annual return for the last 8 years with little variability and set to continue in perpetuity. The original investment of $100 has paid for itself after year 6, generating pure profit for share owners on an ongoing basis after that. The price of a single share has more than doubled since then, with the current market at around $250. This allowed the original owners to lock in more than 100% appreciation on top of the dividends' already healthy gains.

Entropia Universe: Planet Arkadia deeds

In 2014 a new planet within Entropia Universe, Planet Arkadia, announced Arkadia Underground Deeds' offering, making it the world's first $1,000,000 virtual property. The offer allows players to share in the revenues and receive dividends daily. This offering was priced at $5/share with 200,000 made available. The investment has seen consistent daily payouts with over 60% in capital gain since launch, with the share price trading at $7.

Value metrics: Yield, Capital appreciation, Liquidity, Payout stability, Track record length

Yield: Assuming that we are comfortable with the core platform not going away (as discussed in the real estate section), understanding the expected yield or profit on the security, as well as the method of its derivation, is key. We can look at the yield based on the current payout yield (last periodic payment/price of full security), as well as the average long-term yield (average yield / average price over a period) to get an understanding of the absolute levels of profitability expected, and afterward evaluate each trend to gauge likely future direction.

Capital appreciation: This is the second component of potential future profits. It needs to be examined in conjunction with security trading volume trends to understand past dynamics and future potential. This value is a function of the yield, but also of the scarcity of the underlying securities. As investors may be forecasting future payout amount increases, they will drive up the share's value, depressing the current yield but providing a higher future exit value. Anecdotally, this dynamic has played out several times across multiple deeds, with the best ones returning 2X in 6 months.

Liquidity: This metric looks at the size of the specific deed market over the past day, week and month to estimate the speed with which an investment can be liquidated in order to lock in gains or simply to cash out. As this is a rather specialized and captive market, knowing what amounts can be comfortably disposed of via in-game auction houses or via trades between avatars arranged in chat or on forums is a key risk management tactic. While auction history can be easily accessed, estimating the size of market driven by offline negotiations is tougher, but can be glimpsed by examining trading sections of main forums.

Payout stability: The stability or growth of the actual absolute value of periodic payouts is necessary to understand to comfortably predict future cash flows to be reinvested, withdrawn or otherwise deployed. Obtaining historical data on these numbers may prove a bit challenging, but there are usually dedicated players who maintain accurate and meticulous databases with this data.

Track record length: The ability to evaluate investment potential over long periods adds an important degree of comfort. This will not be possible for newer games or newly issued shares and cannot be part of consideration. Established securities have a lot of data to review and analyze; this adds to the likelihood that an investor will be able to accurately estimate future returns and reduce the risk of the investment.

INVENTORY FINANCING

Inventory financing is a type of short-term borrowing option that business owners use to purchase inventory on credit to be repaid after a product is sold. This funding option's core benefits are twofold: enabling higher sales of popular products and creating stockpiles necessary for seasonal businesses. Small- to medium-sized firms can strategically build excess supply, as they know from past experience and customer orders that they are able to sell more inventory if they had more product available. However, they normally don't have the cash on hand to purchase or manufacture the inventory for sale. Seasonal businesses have a slightly different use of funds profile. They need to acquire the necessary inventory to prepare for the busy season, but do not have cash on hand to make a big inventory purchase. Typically, their inventory serves as collateral for the loan. In case of default, those assets are turned over to the lender in lieu of payment. In some instances, the business owner's personal guarantee or a group of owners is also added to make the transaction more secure and lower risk for the investor.

There are multiple platforms out there that provide inventory financing services to businesses. However, their business models do not include crowdfunding these transactions, and thus while certainly viable options for the borrowers, they do not tap into a small investor base to provide capital. The best (and so far, the only) option I have seen that allows purchasing a fractional interest in inventory financing is Kickfurther (www.kickfurther.com). Investors on Kickfurther are technically buying inventory on consignment and own the products they helped fund until they are sold by the brand through their existing sales channels, investors themselves via web store provided, or other Kickfurther users.

Launched in 2015, Kickfurther takes a unique approach to crowdfunding. Instead of raising money from backers in return for equity, the retailer offers a rate of return specified in advance. They also receive a timeframe in which inventory will be sold, when the investors will be paid back their principal, and the agreed-upon profit margin. All backers also get their own web storefront in which they can sell the inventory they just helped finance.

The platform has a rather lengthy and rigorous screening process that assesses each deal's attractiveness. It gives investors a fair degree of insight into the possible risks inherent in a particular transaction. Extensive due diligence is conducted on various aspects of the deal, with the key ones being market analysis, sales and profit history and reporting, operational history, supply chain, inventory shelf life, and credit verification. Other useful indicators of success are existing PO's (purchase orders) to cover the inventory, the history of multiple successfully funded coops, and the relatively small size of inventory-backed loans relative to firm revenues.

Value metrics: Revenue trend, Track record, Deal history, Credit enhancements, Deal size, Timeframe, Yield

Revenue trend: A first step in evaluating the feasibility of investing in inventory is determining how likely the company is to sell the product. Looking at the revenue metrics for prior years, the pattern you want to see is a steady but ideally rapid increase in YOY (year on year) sales numbers. As long as the data is documented and verifiable, a clear upward revenue trajectory is an important variable to consider in making a decision.

Track record: There are two separate areas to pay attention to here: the length of time the company has been in existence and the extent and quality of social media following it has. The reason for reviewing how long the company has existed is to make sure it is a viable and growing business. More importantly, to ensure that you are not working with a start-up entity. That dramatically changes the risk profile for the worse, as you are assuming more significant incremental risks due to a high degree of uncertainty. The diversity and quality of a social media following give an objective, independent proof of the size of current and potential customer base, as well as points to the fact that a company is effectively and actively utilizing multiple channels to advertise and promote its product.

Deal history: One of the interesting features of the platform is that the majority of companies that use it once tend to use it over and over again. As a result, they build a platform-specific track record of success in terms of both deal quality and payback timeliness. By examining the number of deals a business has funded on the platform, and seeing how many were completed successfully (obviously, the metric here is 100%) and on time is a powerful tool to estimate the likelihood of the investment's profitability.

Credit enhancement: There are multiple deal-specific and borrower-specific riders that make the deal less risky and, therefore, more appealing to investors. Some of the core ones are the existence of a PO (purchase order) from a customer covering the entire consignment, payments going directly to suppliers from the platform, the ability to inspect inventory and warehouses, and a personal guarantee of the business owner or owners. All these make various aspects of the transaction safer and less prone to failure or manipulation. Thus, the presence of some or ideally all of them is a desirable and valuable feature.

Deal size: The amount of money the company is looking to borrow should be in line with its past sales track record and not be a large portion of overall revenues. Ideally, a company is funding a specific product or product line that has sold well in the past, and it has many sales of other products, so that the batch being financed represents 10% or less of the overall prior year's sales volume.

Timeframe: The longer the payback time is, the longer the funds are tied up, and longer maturities require higher annualized rates of compensation to be desirable and as compensation for the lack of liquidity. The time premium can be several percentage points on an annual basis, but if the deal timeline corresponds precisely to a specific order or campaign, the effect of the timeframe risk is diminished. Most co-ops on the platform are in the range of 2-6 months, meaning the funds can be cycled several times a year. The speed of repayment reduces the risk profile of the transaction, as the funds are at risk for shorter time periods, and cycling them allows investors to take advantage of a more diverse set of opportunities.

Yield: This is likely the first metric people look at when evaluating a deal. Ultimately, what matters is how profitable the deal is. The magnitude of the deal's yield is a function of all the metrics discussed above, and in fact, can be treated as a proxy for a combined metric score. Yields range from 10% annualized on the low end to 20+% annualized for longer risk deals. Of course, the yield value means nothing if the borrower wholly or partially defaults. Then it needs to be adjusted by recovery amount and will most likely be negative.

INCOME SHARE AGREEMENTS

An income share agreement (or ISA) is a financial structure in which an individual or organization provides a fixed amount of money to a recipient who, in exchange, agrees to pay back a percentage of their income for a specified period of time. They can function like non-voting shares in a company where the recipient is treated like a company.

Sports

Income share agreements in the sports world allow investors and enthusiasts to use their knowledge to participate in revenue streams generated by individual athletes or sports teams they love.

For athletes, the terms usually specify that an investor gets a defined percentage of future on-field, on-court, on-course, or on-ice earnings for a defined period OR fixed contributions from the athlete for a defined period. For sports teams, the investment is an equity ownership. The revenue share is based on the whole team's performance instead of an individual player, which takes away many idiosyncratic risks.

For thoroughbreds, the investment is in an equity share in a corporation with direct ownership of a horse or horses. This entitles the investor to the agreed-upon percentage of all earnings from races, stud fees, and other revenue streams. At the end of a racehorse's earnings life or if the horse is sold, the corporation will be liquidated, and shareholders at that time will receive a final dividend. This approach is similar to the one covered in the Bloodstock investment chapter covered in the next section and represents an alternative way to access the revenue streams from the space.

Companies like SportBLX https://www.sportblx.com/ create fractional interests in either the athlete's earnings or the team's or holding corporation's equity. The shares are then offered on the SportBLX platform and can subsequently be bought and sold as investors change their views and rebalance their portfolios.

Value metrics: Income share percentage, Payment cap, Repayment term, Track record

Income share percentage: Understanding what the percentage of income represents in dollar terms is the key to determining whether the share price makes sense. The dollar amounts of future payments require the absolute level of future revenues to be estimated. The attractiveness of the deal hinges upon whether the percentage offered is well justified and likely to be profitable. It is also important to clearly specify whether the revenue sharing is on the gross income or whether some costs are being netted against the gross, and the percentage is calculated off of the adjusted number. In this case, the percentage should be higher than if based on gross numbers.

Payment cap: Assuming that the payments under contract are pari passu with the team or athlete's revenues, setting the upper limit of the payback (if it is set at all) will significantly impact the contract's future profitability in cases when performance is solid and growing. There is latitude in the multiples determined in the contract (2X, 3X) as well as two-tier solutions where after an agreed-upon multiple has been received, the investor is still entitled to future cash flows, but at a lower rate.

Repayment term: The contractual length of the term during which the investor continues to share revenue is the defining metric of the contract. The longer the time horizon, with perpetuity being the extreme case, the more income accrues to the investor, and the more valuable the equity participation is. While the term is usually capped at the 5 to 10-year mark, multiple variations exist, allowing the savvy investor to benefit from good analysis and projection skills.

Track record: While past results do not guarantee future ones, they are still the best available estimate at a point in time of the potential magnitude of future success. Observing steady growth, or even accelerating one in the player's or teams' key sports statistics, winning percentages, and popularity, which translates into more lucrative future contracts, can allow an investor to extrapolate the track record and create future performance projections based on it. These data-based projections are the key to calculating the expected value of the deal.

Student Loans

College ISAs as an idea have their roots in a 1955 essay by famed economist Milton Friedman that explored the potential of investing in "human capital" by paying for education. While formal ISA programs have gained steam recently, they are still relatively uncommon.

ISAs have gained prominence as an alternative to the traditional student loan system in American higher education. Several private companies now offer ISAs for various purposes, including as a funding source for college tuition. Instead of taking out a loan, students agree to pay a percentage of their future earnings for a fixed number of months. ISA obligations can be ended earlier by making prepayments.

The key driver of an ISA investment is the potential employment outcome of the students. Because investors are getting a share of the students' earnings, they earn greater returns if students have good employment outcomes. Evaluating schools' historical outcomes is essential, as they give important clues for future performance (although past performance is no guarantee of future returns). ISAs are not credit-based.

Several investment platforms sprung up over the last few years, with some like Upstart (www.upstart.com) pivoting to a classical student loan framework. Currently, investors can access the ISA's via several platforms, some of the better known being https://www.edly.co/ and https://mentorworks.com/.

Value metrics: Income share percentage, Projected salary, Salary floor, Payment cap, Repayment term, Geography

Income share percentage: The percentage of the borrower's gross income is the key metric, which, combined with projected salary levels, can be used to project the size of future monthly cash flows. College ISAs typically have income shares between 2 and 10 percent.

Projected salary: This is the estimate of expected future salary based on the school reputation, selected major and geographic location, amongst others. The expected future field of work, determined mainly by the subjects focused on in school, is a key determinant of the expected income levels and their stability and longevity and allows the investor to rather accurately estimate the future stream of cash flows and evaluate the likelihood of the deal being profitable, or at least breaking even. Evaluating the absolute value of the salary allows the investor to estimate a range of risks: the probability of it being below the salary floor clause, probability of the payments over the repayment term being less than the original loan, and the probability that the expected interest will not be paid within the ISA timeframe.

Salary floor: This is a fundamental covenant in the agreement, as this directly affects the probability of future payback of principal, as well as any interest. An ISA's salary floor reflects the student's expected post-graduate income. If it stays below the floor for extended periods of time, the attractiveness of the deal for the lender is greatly diminished, as there is a high likelihood that little or no cash will be recovered. As a result, the floor level needs to be set very carefully, taking into account the expected future field of work, geography and the length of the repayment period. It is crucial to calibrate this key covenant of the ISA, such as salary floor, to fairly reflect the different living wages required in various cities. This varies widely across the nation, often drastically. A $50,000 income may provide a high standard of living in Wyoming but would be quite inadequate in New York City.

Payment cap: This specifies the most a borrower would have to repay under the ISA. The payment cap is a function of the amount initially received by the borrower, with the typical cap being two times the amount borrowed.

With caps above 2X borrowed, as well as ISAs that don't have a payment cap at all, a borrower could repay far more than they got over the repayment period, providing much better returns for the investor.

Repayment term: This clause stipulates how long the ISA contract lasts. Repayment terms typically range from 2 years (24 months) to 10 years (120 months). Some ISAs will count months in which you earn less than the salary floor toward your repayment term. Others extend the repayment term in these instances, with the latter being the preferred method for the investor.

Geography: It is important to calibrate the key covenants of the ISA, such as the before mentioned salary floor and income share percentage, to reflect the different living wages required in various cities. Ensuring that the terms reasonably accommodate the borrower's actual needs helps ensure an uninterrupted future repayment stream and a favorable situation for both parties to the contract.

BLOODSTOCK

The term "bloodstock" refers to horses of thoroughbred breed best known for their use in horse racing. The thoroughbred as it is known today was developed in 17th and 18th century England, when native mares were crossbred with imported Oriental stallions of Arabian, Barb, and Turkoman breeding. All modern thoroughbreds can trace their pedigrees to three stallions originally imported into England in the 17th and 18th centuries, and to a larger number of foundation mares of primarily English breeding. During the 18th and 19th centuries, the thoroughbred breed spread throughout the world; they were imported into North America starting in 1730 and into Australia, Europe, Japan and South America during the 19th century. Millions of Thoroughbreds exist today, and around 100,000 foals are registered each year worldwide.

The typical thoroughbred ranges from 15.2 to 17.0 hands (62 to 68 inches, 157 to 173 cm) high, averaging 16 hands (64 inches, 163 cm). They are most often bay, dark bay, or brown, chestnut, black, or gray. Less common colors recognized in the United States include roan (even a mixture of colored and white hairs on the body) and palomino (gold coat with white mane and tail). White is very rare but is a recognized color separate from gray. Good-quality thoroughbreds have a well-chiseled head on a long neck, high withers (the highest part of a horse's back, lying at the base of the neck above the shoulders: the height of a horse is measured to the withers), a deep chest, a short back, good depth of hindquarters, a lean body, and long legs.

Unlike a significant number of registered breeds today, a horse cannot be registered as a thoroughbred with The Jockey Club registry unless conceived by live cover, the witnessed natural mating of a mare and a stallion. The main reason is that a stallion has a limited number of mares serviced by live cover. This prevents an oversupply of thoroughbreds and preserves the high prices paid for horses of the finest or most popular lineages.

Beyond the initial price of purchasing a horse, which on average is $60,000 and can quickly rise to seven figures, expenses for maintaining and training a competitive racehorse amount to $50,000+ annually, not including vet and travel costs. Buying a share of a racehorse or shares of multiple horses via various partnerships or online platforms such as https://myracehorse.com, https://www.westpointtb.com/, https://eclipsetbpartners.com/ or https://www.jamierailton.com/ can help investors mitigate risk while still capturing the desired upside. When you own a fraction of a horse, you only have to worry about a fraction of the maintenance costs. You also enjoy a much more diversified and thus de-risked portfolio of colts, where chances of the group getting prize money are quite high as an aggregate. There's more than $1 billion in purse prizes annually for racehorses, and each year 2% of horses win $125,000, 4% win $100,000, and 6% win $90,000. The investor becomes a part of an investment vehicle with a 12–14-month maturity date, at which time all the horses in the package are sold.

Beyond racing, male horses have extra value through resale, syndication as a stallion and stud fee earnings for breeding. Tapit, the top American sire, earns $300,000 for stud fees, and 2015 Triple Crown winner America Pharaoh, the first horse to win the Grand Slam of Thoroughbred racing, earns $200,000. Even less significant stallions can be bred for $1,000 and up. Female horses can earn money by racing, resale and producing foals that can be sold as yearlings. Because fillies can all produce foals, they have residual value as producers and, as such, are a safer investment.

Value metrics: Body, Pedigree, Potential, Track record

Body: Characteristics including a well-balanced body, front legs that point forward with no deviation on the joints or feet and an athletic walk are the key parameters that allow the investor to estimate a horse's raw potential

Pedigree: Horses sired by a famous colt and therefore endowed with a superior genetic potential to be successful is a tremendous boon to value, as great genes have been shown to significantly increase the probability of racing success

Potential: The horse's size and scope, which refers to a horse's ability to develop and grow, together with Body and Pedigree, form the defining set of physical characteristics from which the likelihood of future success can be reasonably estimated.

Track record: An accomplished racehorse is much less risky, because its class level is established. It can and should earn racing income. A long solid track record of success, especially at the highest levels, is a great contributor to value and holds great promise for continued excellence. Of course, that comes with a premium in price. Prices for the upper echelon of Triple Crown prospects range from $600,000 to $10 million after they have shown elite ability.

POKER PLAYERS

Professional poker is a straightforward game of winners and losers, with hundreds of millions of dollars being paid out in prizes annually. The Main Event of the WSOP (World Series of Poker) is the game's biggest annual competition that alone attracted 8,569 entries and had a prize pool of over $80MM, with the winner getting $10MM. In 2014 about 50% of the players of the WSOP likely received financial support from past and current players, family members and other poker investors. Today, as much as 80% of the players in the tournament have financial backing.

There is a lot of precedent for past winners selling shares in their "action," i.e., their potential winnings. In 2004 Greg Raymer won the World Series of Poker Main Event and paid out more than $2 million out of his $5 million prize (40%) to those who had invested in him. The world-famous Daniel Negreanu reportedly sold 13% of his action before coming second in the 2014 Big One for One Drop. Known as "staking," the practice of financially backing players for a cut of their winnings is a growing business. Staking players has also expanded beyond poker to bowling, golf, tennis, drone racing and even e-sports.

Many big-money tournaments have "buy-ins" (entry fees) that can be prohibitively expensive for some players to take part in. Most players would rather swap some of their potential winnings in exchange for significantly reducing or completely removing the upfront expense. Done with written contracts, staking usually involves paying the "buy-ins" to tournaments over the course of a year in exchange for a percentage of the player's earnings. The agreement includes a number of clauses specifying all aspects of training and play, such as the number of games to be played, the cut, when the profits should be split, how much coaching there will be (if any), and how many games per day, week or month the player should play. Players with good track records can charge an extra fee on top of the base share price for the privilege of backing them, a practice called "mark-up."

In long-term poker backing arrangements, players are often required to pay "makeup." This means all their buy-ins are tallied as debt that must be repaid from future winnings before the player can participate in the upside. The most common deal is 50/50 plus make-up. This translates to the financial backer paying for the total cost of the poker player's tournament entry and should the player win, they split the profit. For example, say the entry fee is $2,000, and the player wins $20,000, the backer gets straight back the $2,000, and both parties split the $18,000. Deals like this cannot be beneficial for a player who goes on a losing streak. They can rack up buy-in debts, and "make-up" has to be earned by the player and returned to the backer before receiving their share of the winning. So, if the player keeps playing without winning and racks up a total of $40,000 in make-up, the player would need to win $50,000 to take $5,000 home ($40,000 is paid to the backer, and the $10,000 profit is split 50/50).

Many sites match up investors with players or work on the now well-established crowd funding model. YouStake and Two Plus Two are among the most widely used, and offer some attractive features to make the process more transparent and formalized. They provide a worldwide forum for bringing players and investors together, and vetting each side to ensure both are legitimate and capable of performing as agreed. They also include contractual agreements, which have previously been lacking in the often informal nature of poker backing and staking, often relying on gentleman's agreements and a handshake.

Two Plus Two live marketplace (https://forumserver.twoplustwo.com/) is a lot like Craig's List and other online forums. The site allows investors to negotiate with individual poker players looking for backers to stake them in tournaments. It is a great option for exploring the space, because many of the players are simply looking for staking in a single tournament, and some investors do not have to wait an entire season for players to repay them. A player posts his or her request for staking and sells shares of the winnings to backers. There is a wide range of amateur online poker players and even professionals on the forum selling shares of their potential winnings to investors.

YouStake platform (https://youstake.com/marketplace) is an option for poker players and investors looking to stake players. The site brings in a third-party platform that helps to match qualified players with investors. It helps take the pressure off investors from having to deal directly with players and set up contracts for payments.

Value metrics: Discipline, Prior personal experience, Character, In-form

Discipline: A player with a solid work ethic, even temperament, solid training, and game discipline is the kind that backers want to stake.

Prior personal experience: In many cases, players are chosen because the investor is a poker player himself and has played against their potential investee themselves. There is no substitute for direct personal experience, and the ability to recognize equal or greater talent in the opponent can lead to truly well-informed decisions.

Character: This is the behavioral track record of the player, and must be taken very seriously, as no amount of skill can compensate for lack of reliability, poor reputation, or outright known instances of dishonesty. Conducting extensive due diligence via interviews with prior stakers, other players, and general industry insiders can allow the investor to determine if the player is trustworthy, i.e., that he has honored his commitments to prior investors or whether he "rolled" (ran with money) in the past. If a player caused various problems for other investors, it is important to understand what kind and why, and walk away if there is a bad behavior trend.

In-form / on a roll: Staking players is best done based on their most recent performance, not necessarily their overall reputation. Researching players on sites like Sharkscope that tracks tournament results is an excellent way to find someone on a "hot streak." Experts suggest picking a player "in form" with a proven track record over a couple thousand games and up at least a few thousand dollars. These are the players that are "on a roll" or "hot." They often win consecutively more than a player who is in a slump. Be wary of the guys where all their money came from one big score.

MUSIC ROYALTIES

Historically music royalty transactions took place in private and were available only to industry insiders. The surging popularity of streaming services, which let users listen to an unlimited amount of music, reshaped the music industry and made song catalogs more valuable. Streaming revenue rose 34% in 2018 and has injected new life into an industry that had revenue declines from 2001 to 2014. The sector is expected to double by 2030 to $131 billion from 2017 levels. Millennials and GenZ's are spending more of their annual budgets on music, and there is a growing penetration of streaming on smartphones, especially in the emerging markets.

Investors have shown increasing interest in acquiring song catalogs as streaming platforms from Spotify, Apple Inc. and others add premium subscribers. Music-royalties funds often buy rights from lower-profile songwriters who collaborate with global superstars and are better incentivized to cash in part of their rights to future earnings. While music-royalties funds tend to attract institutional investors, online marketplaces such as Royalty Exchange (https://www.royaltyexchange.com) and SongVest (https://www.songvest.com/) allow individuals to buy slices of song catalogs in transactions that are typically far smaller.

Though the songs being put on the auction block are often famous, the actual rights holders' names are usually not. The "ecosystem" surrounding the artists whose names are attached to the hits includes a large group of behind-the-scenes people, such as professional songwriters, managers, producers, studio musicians and independent labels and music publishers, who are not able to raise capital by going on tour or signing a new publishing deal with an advance. Regular musicians find it hard to raise the capital they need to kick-start their career or even push it along. They seek out other ways to raise cash, with their royalties becoming a potential immediate earner for them.

Most auctions give the winner the rights to 10 years of future payments, while a few offer payments for the full artist's lifetime, plus 70 years after that. Big-name artists attract a premium price for their royalties, expressed as a larger "multiple" of last year's earnings.

Royalties derive from album sales, radio play, online streaming, TV and movie rights, or any combination of these, depending on the individual auction terms. There are several types of royalties such as **mechanical**, based on the number of recordings sold and given to the songwriter, producer, and recording artists, **synchronization,** when music is used in connection to visual images such as TV adverts, films, video games and TV programs and **performance,** which earns money when music is performed publicly through broadcast on television, radio and TV.

Value metrics: Artist, Remaining life, Clauses, Usage

Artist: The artist's popularity affects the value of the royalty stream, as the more popular the song is, the more it is played, and the more money it will potentially make. While material from top artists is likely to command higher prices, it is also a much safer bet. From a risk/reward perspective, it is a good indicator of the likelihood of profit.

Remaining life: Studies of music as a capital asset have indicated that 75% of the expected royalty income occurs during the first year after the release. It subsequently depreciates at a 10% annual rate between years one and five, and then approaches near-zero. This means that often by the time a royalty is made available for sale, most of the immediate income has already been generated for the musical asset owner. The seller hopes that an optimistic buyer will overestimate the total value of the revenue stream, relying on first-year data as a reliable indicator of future sales.

Clauses: The value of the purchase is also greatly affected by the extent to which it permits the sellers of royalties to utilize the "buyback option" clause reserving the right to purchase sold royalty at 125% of the purchase price at any time within five years, effectively giving the seller an option to capture all the upside and offload all of the risk onto the buyer.

Usage: Holiday-specific songs can make a lot of money over a long period of time because they are played over and over every year. A media tie-in, where a song is used in a soundtrack of a famous movie or show and becomes closely associated with it, increases the likelihood that cash will be generated. Other uses include mobile ringtones, stage productions, print music, toys and other novelty items.

INVESTMENT PLATFORMS

Whisky cask investments

https://www.whiskyinvestdirect.com/

https://whiskeywealthclub.com/

https://www.cask88.com/

https://www.rarewhisky101.com/barrel-brokerage

En primeur wine

https://www.wineinvestment.com/

https://www.vinovest.co/

Web assets

https://onfolio.co

Virtual financial assets

https://www.planetcalypso.com/

https://www.decentraland.org

Inventory financing

www.kickfurther.com

Income share agreements

https://www.sportblx.com/

https://www.edly.co/

https://mentorworks.com/

Bloodstock

https://myracehorse.com

https://www.westpointtb.com/

https://eclipsetbpartners.com/

https://www.jamierailton.com/

Poker players

https://forumserver.twoplustwo.com/

https://youstake.com/marketplace

Music royalties

https://www.royaltyexchange.com

https://www.songvest.com

Fractional revenue shares metric summary

Table 1

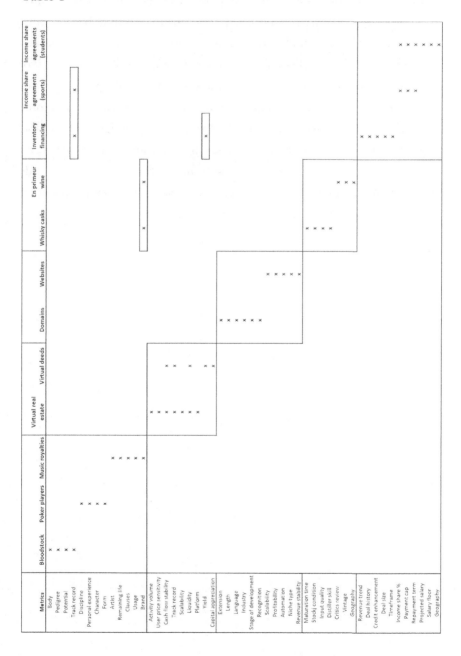

The degree to which the key drivers differ so drastically among the various fractional revenue share categories further underscores the extreme importance of having strong subject matter expertise across various subcategories of assets. Five main groupings of category types share similar frameworks and evaluation approaches: performance revenue shares, virtual assets, web assets, alcohol and income share agreements. Developing checklists, standalone evaluation analytics, and comparison metrics for all of the above is necessary, but time-consuming and challenging even for investment professionals. It is absolutely possible to study hard and become enough of a subject matter expert on your own by pulling from multiple disparate sources of information and setting up your own analytics and portfolios. For those interested in a faster, more efficient and ready-made system, I invite you to take the course on fractional revenue shares on www.michaelfoxrabinovitz.com/courses.

COLLECTIBLES

In writing my previous bestselling book, *Own a Fraction, Earn a Fortune: The Complete Guide to Co-investing in Art and Collectibles*, I focused entirely on fractional investment in a wide range of collectible assets, but due to several considerations, some asset classes were left out. While this book's core purpose is to get the reader acquainted with the fractional revenue investment set, I feel it is important to present the fantastic set of more unusual, esoteric and less known collectibles that did not make it into the first book. I am certain that both returning readers and those who are new will find this section just as useful, informative and captivating as the first one.

FOSSILS

Since the beginning of recorded history, fossils have confounded their discoverers, leading to wild folktales about mythical dragons and other strange creatures. Our collective fascination with dinosaurs dates back at least 2,000 years, when Chinese writings described what were thought to be dragon bones. In the 17th century, an English scientist theorized that a dinosaur thigh bone was from a human giant.

Century later, naturalists Carl Linnaeus and Charles Darwin established the foundations of modern paleontology with taxonomic hierarchies and evolutionary theory. Thanks to the invention of radiometric dating in the early nineteenth century, and the discovery of countless fossils, we now have a more thorough picture of the incredible story of life on Earth than we could ever have imagined, and it continues to expand. According to National Geographic, over 50 new species of dinosaurs are still being discovered every year.

Many enthusiasts fall into the world of fossils through their interest in art or other collectibles. Collectors who are bored of buying yet another bottle of wine, watch or supercar are finding fossils an interesting alternative. Dinosaurs are not just part of mainstream culture, but are increasingly prized as art objects as well. While the value of a rare stamp is really only what someone is willing to pay for it, the rarest natural history objects, such as fossils, also hold great scientific value, an objective and measurable quality.

Today's dinosaur collection trend is in part fueled by the generation that grew up watching the movies *The Land Before Time* (1988) and *Jurassic Park* (1993). The fossil market boomed in the late 1980s when dealers from Japan started buying up prized fossils for their collections, driving up prices beyond the reach of most educational institutions. What made fossils so valuable is not their potential scientific value or the actual cost of excavating and preparing them, but the desire of their new owner (and the competing bidders) to say, "Look what I bought!"

55

A growing number of wealthy individuals have taken an interest in buying dinosaurs for their private collections. People love the combination of popular science, popular history, and the excitement of breaking new ground. Fossils are items of undoubted scientific interest and thus have an intrinsic value dependent on their value to science, but like shells and butterflies, they are collected and displayed as much for their beauty as for their scientific interest, much as one would buy a sculpture or a painting. Large ammonites and slabs of petrified wood are made into coffee tables, and one company lets people decorate their kitchen or bathroom with tiles made from Green River shale, each with a fossil fish in the middle.

The least expensive type of dinosaur fossil is coprolite or fossilized dinosaur dung. It's more decorative than it sounds and usually costs about $20 to $50. Even more popular and still very affordable are dinosaur eggs, at $400 to $1,500. At the next price level, dinosaur skulls range from about $25,000 to $100,000. Complete skeletons are the most expensive, from a minimum of $200,000 to the record price of over $30 million paid for the T-rex named Stan.

An idea common to every speculative bubble since the tulip mania in 17th century Holland is that the buying and selling of the rare object is also a way to make money. Thus, some of the fossils purchased over the past decade make their way back to the auction houses at greatly inflated prices. The value of rare, museum-quality fossils is quickly rising, as important fossils disappear from the research community into private collections at prices well beyond the means of public museums to match. By the time many collectors will catch on to what is happening, the best opportunities to acquire new material will be gone. A very finite population of truly fine grade and authentic fossils will simply change hands from one collection to another at insane prices.

The field of rare collectibles, fossils and artifacts exhibits an ever-increasing demand and international appeal that transcends all countries, languages and cultures. Fossil collecting is becoming mainstream, evidenced by the surge in major international natural history auctions. It is likely to rank amongst the most promising future investments in collectibles regarding the rarest and finest examples. New paleontological discoveries also have the potential to affect the desire for the specimens. For instance, if Triceratops were suddenly discovered to have really been vicious carnivores and not gentle herbivores, as is the current theory, these specimens' desirability would likely increase as a result.

The highest quality and rarest fossils' value goes up each and every year, as they are simply not making fossils anymore. Minerals, gems, natural precious metal specimens and meteorites are still forming in the Earth or dropping from the sky. Still, unlike these collectibles, where the supply keeps growing, there is a finite number of fossils on the planet. Not only are deposits becoming rapidly exhausted, but many states and entire countries pass legislation each year banning the collecting and export of fossils. The ever-increasing expansion of infrastructure projects along with new commercial and residential development continues to destroy former prime collecting sites and areas.

The rare collectible market offers a haven for investing if done wisely and only in the finest and rarest specimens. No venue of this field has more promise than that of collecting rare fossils. The fastest and most promising appreciation in value will be for the unadulterated, authentic fossil specimens of the absolute finest quality and rarest types sourced from highly competent and extremely knowledgeable professional dealers well-versed in all lab techniques of conservation, preparation, restoration and repair.

The Internet made fossils significantly easier to find and compare and greatly increased the number of sellers and buyers in the marketplace. Buyers now gather price information from greater numbers of potential sellers without incurring a significant cost. This mitigates any potential supply monopolies and brings greater competition to the marketplace as sellers now compete with each other—not just regionally, but nationally and even internationally.

Although only about a half-dozen dinosaur skeletons go on the auction block each year, interest in collecting fossils is booming, with prices rising astronomically as buyers vie for the top specimens at auctions and in galleries. Prominent bone collectors Nicolas Cage and Leonardo DiCaprio have both made headlines with their purchases. Still, many of the new crop of big-spending collectors are based in Asia: secretive connoisseurs from China, Hong Kong, Taiwan, Thailand, Singapore, Indonesia and the Philippines have collectively spent tens of millions of US dollars on fossils over the past decade.

Their purchases would not be out of place in "Crazy Rich Asians." One collector in Singapore has a woolly mammoth tusk taking pride of place in his living room. A devotee in Hong Kong is rumored to own a pterodactyl, and an enthusiast in Taiwan has an enormous skeleton of a duck-billed prosaurolophus, which at 11 meters long is the length of roughly two cars. In 2016, an allosaurus named Kan sold for €1.1 million. In 2017, a mammoth skeleton was sold to a private collector for €548,250, and in 2018 two dinosaur skeletons—one allosaurus, one diplodocus—were sold together for nearly €3 million.

Deep-pocketed buyers can almost always outbid museums, and institutions are losing out to individuals all the time. Museums simply don't have the same kind of liquidity that wealthy private collectors do, and that immediate access to cash is what makes the difference. The only way for museums to get access to the top specimens is to get those people on their boards. However, as a counterargument, some private collectors believe that the market for dinosaur bones has helped reinvigorate interest in fossils and paleontology, leading to more discoveries.

The U.S. is unique in its property laws. Although anything on federal land belongs to the government, fossils discovered on privately owned lands are private property, where anybody can dig for fossils with the landowner's permission. But even then, custody battles over dinosaur remains are not uncommon. In early 2020, the Montana Supreme Court ruled in a landmark case that dinosaur fossils are not classified as minerals after an ongoing legal battle over the ownership of dinosaur bones found on a ranch where the surface and mineral rights were owned by different people.

If you find a dinosaur skeleton under the right conditions, you can do pretty much whatever you want with it—including, of course, selling it however you please, such as a baby T-rex that has been put on eBay a few years ago. Digging for dinosaur fragments is a big business. Local buffs routinely search for bones, and dinosaur expeditions are a top tourist attraction, with several locations, like the Wyoming Dinosaur Center in Thermopolis, offering amateurs the chance to participate in excavations for a fee.

There's never been a fossilized penis or vagina found on a dinosaur, and the first person who finds one is going to make bundles of cash. The dinosaur penis would be roughly equivalent to an early Picasso that turned up in the estate of a woman who was the artist's secret lover and received the painting directly from him, with documentation that proved everything.

The aforementioned "finders-keepers" principle, however, only applies to fossils discovered on private property. Fossils unearthed on state, federal or tribal land must be turned over to the respective authorities. Fossils are protected on federally owned lands such as the National Parks by the Paleontological Resources Preservation Act of 2009.

In the U.S, the largest quantity of fossils has been unearthed in California, Wyoming and Montana, with Oklahoma, Utah and the Dakotas not far behind. These are some of the richest repositories of dinosaur fossils in the world. By contrast, seven states – Kentucky, Iowa, Minnesota, New Hampshire, Rhode Island, Vermont, and Wisconsin – have no dinosaur fossils, because they were mostly below sea level during the dinosaur era and didn't have the right kind of sediment to preserve fossils.

International rules and regulations impacting fossil collection, sales and export are murky at best – and are often ignored. Since 1924 Mongolia has declared all fossils discovered within the country's borders to be the property of the state. Private collections are banned, and no fossils are allowed to be shipped out of the country without special permission. Legal action has also been taken against auction houses to block the sale of stolen Mongolian fossils. However, that didn't stop many entrepreneurial archeologists from smuggling quite a few of them out of the country, presumably selling them directly to private collectors.

Most major museums in Europe and the United States have strict rules about acquiring looted fossils. Institutions like the American Museum of Natural History have sponsored expeditions to Mongolia with government approval to temporarily remove fossils for study. But most of the dinosaur specimens from Mongolia (and China, which also enacted a law requiring government permission to export fossils) that routinely show up for sale around the world have been transported illegally. The *China Daily* newspaper reported that over three years, China reclaimed more than 5,000 fossil specimens from foreign countries, including Australia, the United States, Canada and Italy.

In 2013, actors Nicholas Cage and Leonardo DiCaprio reportedly got into a bidding war over the 67-million-year-old skull of a Tyrannosaurus bataar. DiCaprio was outbid by Cage on a rare Tyrannosaurus bataar skull that Cage bought for $276,000. However, Cage agreed to return it to the Mongolian government after investigators determined that it had been smuggled out of Mongolia and shouldn't have left the country in the first place.

If obtained or sold under the wrong circumstances, dinosaur bones can land the seller in serious trouble. In 2012, Eric Prokopi, a commercial paleontologist from Florida, was convicted of smuggling a T. rex skeleton into the U.S. from Mongolia, where dinosaur fossils are considered state property. It was seized by U.S. authorities before it could be auctioned off, and Prokopi spent three months in federal prison.

Even when a sale itself was perfectly legal, a buyer can be hurt by a transaction that involves outright forgery, misrepresented restorations or improper identification. Techniques used today to forge and fabricate items have become so sophisticated that it becomes dangerous "guesswork" without current and continual experience. Many dealers have been sold forgeries by their suppliers who they thought were "trustworthy" only to find out the truth at their customers' expense and reputation.

Outright fakes are sometimes easy to spot. Other times, they are nearly impossible to expose without special equipment, regardless of experience. Microscopic examination with a 10-30x power binocular microscope is usually sufficient, provided you know what you are looking for.

A fake most often overlooked is when expert forgers mix the real fossils from various sources, like a massive dinosaur tooth or claw that is actually made up of parts from multiple genuine specimens. Other common examples are fossils or artifacts that have much more restoration and repair than is disclosed. Lab cleaning equipment and processes will detect tricks and substances that will fool UV light inspections and even X-ray inspection fraud. Still, most dealers do not have access to this equipment or know what to look for.

Another commonly seen problem is that a fossil or stone tool artifact is incorrectly identified, sometimes due to ignorance and sometimes out of outright malice. Some well-known examples are virtually worthless fossil turtle claws being sold as "raptor" dromaeosaur dinosaur claws and Carcharodontosaurus dinosaur teeth being sold as "African T. rex" teeth, even though the Tyrannosaurus rex never lived in Africa.

One of the best-known fakes in the history of paleontology is the "Piltdown Man," a sophisticated scientific fraud involving early hominid remains found near Piltdown village in Sussex, England, in 1912 by an amateur archaeologist Charles Dawson. He claimed to have discovered the 'missing link' between ape and man. Arthur Smith Woodward, Keeper of Geology at the Natural History Museum at the time, made a reconstruction of the skull fragments. Based on that, he and other archaeologists hypothesized that the find indicated evidence of a human ancestor living 500,000 years ago.

However, in 1949, new dating technology discovered that not only were the Piltdown remains just 50,000 years old, but more importantly, the skull and jaw fragments actually came from two different species, a human and an ape, probably an orangutan.

The most famous recent hoax in the paleontology community was the so-called "Piltdown Chicken," a reference to the aforementioned Piltdown Man debacle. *National Geographic Magazine* announced the discovery of the Archaeoraptor liaoningensis in China in 1999, celebrated as the missing link between dinosaurs and birds. However, it was later discovered that the fossil had been forged by creating a "composite" combining different parts of different species to create something that looks like a new animal, as was the case with the Piltdown Chicken.

Value Metrics:

Core: Scarcity, Rarity, Provenance, Condition

Unique: Age, Aesthetics, Locality

Scarcity: Not all fossils are scarce; for example, the supply of *Carcharocles megalodon* teeth has increased substantially during the past 20 years. In 1991, the majority of commercially available large shark teeth came from phosphate mines in North Carolina and Florida or a handful of offshore or river sites. By 2011, fossil shark teeth were available not only from these same sources but also from numerous other river deposits and international sources in Chile, Peru, and Italy.

Key items that affect scarcity are the supply and demand of fossils, the appearance of any new sites or dealers flooding the market with certain specimens, or closed sites that would ensure particular specimens won't come into the market anymore.

Rarity: This is driven primarily by the type of dinosaur and how many similar or better-quality specimens exist. Limited supply on the market, combined with few comparable level assets, ensure a strong and growing level of interest in the most unique assets. The rarest form of fossilization is the preservation of original skeletal material and even soft tissue. For example, insects have been preserved perfectly in amber, which is ancient tree sap.

Provenance: With all purchases, it is crucial to get a written guarantee of condition, history of repair and restoration, and a certificate of identification and authenticity, all of which must have no conditions or expiration dates and be issued by the dealer you are buying from. Sourcing from a highly regarded dealer is a must, but even then, there are no true guarantees.

Conventional auctions and other online auctions should be approached with extreme caution. Convincing forgeries, or completely misidentified items, are routinely sold in major and minor auction houses. The auctioneer simply does not have the time and knowledge to vet every single piece going up for auction. As a bidder, you are usually bound by an agreement that states that all sales are final, and the seller or auction house makes no express claim of authenticity or identification.

Condition: Buyers should look at how much is original bone, how much of it was prepared, and if it had to be restored. Minimal restoration, i.e., specimens comprised primarily of original bone/fossil material, is strongly preferred. The specimens should have been excavated and prepared to high standards, exposing the surface details without damage.

The best unbiased advice a buyer can seek is a second opinion from a paleontologist or related scientist affiliated with a local museum. While they may not be fully aware of the techniques for faking fossils, they will know what the real specimen should look like or what the specimen in question may be, if identification is an issue.

Age: All else being equal, the older the specimen is, the more valuable it has the potential to be, given that the fossil type itself is sufficiently scarce and rare. To establish the age of a rock or a fossil, researchers use some type of clock to determine the date it was formed. Geologists commonly use radiometric dating methods, based on the natural radioactive decay of certain elements such as potassium and carbon, as reliable clocks to date ancient events.

There are two accepted ways to determine the age of a dinosaur fossil. One is called relative geologic time, which involves deciding whether one dinosaur fossil is older or younger than another. To determine relative age, one must realize that dinosaur fossils are preserved in layers of sedimentary rock, deposited in sequence, one on top of the other. Fossils contained in an older, lower rock layer are relatively older than fossils contained in a higher, newer layer. The other is often called absolute geologic time, which involves estimating how many millions of years old a dinosaur fossil is.

Aesthetics: Unique and visually appealing specimens are more likely to increase in value, although this criteria is highly subjective. Some might argue that the big teeth and claws of t-rexes and triceratops make them sexier than anything else. Still, some collectors concentrate on other types of fossils entirely, such as shark's teeth or trilobites.

Locality: If a fossil was found at a famous and well-known dig location, this adds additional credibility and scientific clout to a specimen, making it more valuable. Below are 10 of the most famous and important fossil locales from around the world, in no particular order.

Green River Formation, Wyoming, is best known among paleontologists for its superbly preserved fossil fish, as well as fossils of turtles, bats, birds, mammals, snakes, and crocodiles.

Seymour Island, Antarctica, is best known for its disarticulated fish fossils, belonging to the victims of the impact that wiped out the dinosaurs. Other fossils include those belonging to marsupials, proving that these animals originated in South America, crossing over to Australia when both continents were connected through Antarctica.

Ediacara Hills, Australia, give their name to the Ediacaran Period, the first new geological period to be declared in 120 years, when it was approved in

2004. Fossils found here, such as 550- to 600-million-year-old jellyfish, crustaceans, flatworms, echinoderms and trilobite ancestors, have revealed that multicellular maritime life was well-established long before the Cambrian.

Anacleto Formation, Argentina, boasts most of the known fossil sites in South America, dating from the Late Cretaceous some 80 million years ago. It is home to numerous nests of fossilized dinosaur eggs, including eggs and bones belonging to titanosaurs. They were the largest animals to ever walk the Earth and never stopped growing, starting their lives weighing barely 11 pounds and reaching up to 25,000 times their original weight over a 40-year period.

Hell Creek Formation, United States, is arguably the most famous fossil site in the world, spanning areas of Montana, North and South Dakota and Wyoming. Dating from the Late Cretaceous, the rocks here have revealed some of the world's best-known dinosaurs, such as the triceratops, tyrannosaurus rex and ankylosaurus.

Joggins Fossil Cliffs, Canada, is home to one of the world's most important Carboniferous fossil sites. The 310-million-year-old rocks there tell the story of a rainforest world where insects and other arthropods grew to alarming sizes and oxygen levels were so high that forest fires were abundant. Among the many fossils unearthed there are those belonging to arthropleura, a millipede that grew up to 7.5 feet long.

Jurassic Coast, England, is a World Heritage Site that spans 95 miles of coastline and is home to cliffs and rocks documenting an incredible 185 million years of the Earth's history. The coastline's sedimentary layers have yielded countless fossils belonging to plants and animals spanning the entire Mesozoic Era, from about 252 to 66 million years ago.

Red Beds, Texas and Oklahoma, is a site dating from the Early Permian, almost 300 million years ago, that has unearthed fossil remains of dimetrodons and numerous other tetrapods. These reptile-like creatures, often characterized by the large sail-like structures on their backs, were among the dominant megafauna throughout most of the world throughout the Permian.

La Brea Tar Pits, California, discoveries include some of the best-preserved samples of iconic Pleistocene megafauna, such as saber-toothed cats, dire wolves, mammoths and ground sloths. The tar pits claimed the lives of many unlucky animals who got stuck in the sticky substance,

Jiufotang Formation, China, boasts this formation dating from the Early Cretaceous Period around 120 million years ago. The area has yielded fossil remains of feathered dinosaurs, prehistoric birds, early mammals, pterosaurs and crocodile-like choristoderan reptiles.

Top 10 highest priced items:

1-Stan the T-rex: $31.9M

Named after the paleontologist who discovered him, Stan is one of the most complete Tyrannosaurus rex skeletons ever found, one of only about 50 T. rex fossils ever discovered, with most displayed in museums. First discovered by amateur paleontologist Stan Sacrison in 1987 at Hell Creek formation in the US, part of an area known as the Cretaceous Badlands, the bones were initially misidentified as those of a Triceratops. In 1992, visiting paleontologists began to excavate the bones and realized he was, in fact, a Tyrannosaurus rex. The excavation and restoration of the skeleton took a total of 3 years and 30,000 hours to complete, after which he was put on a custom mount and displayed to the public on Hill City's Main Street in South Dakota.

Paleontologists say Stan would have weighed 7 to 8 tons at his peak and showed signs of a difficult and violent life. He suffered a broken neck, with two of his vertebrae bonding together and a third immobilized. He also had a puncture in his skull and ribs. It is one of the most complete T. rex fossils ever found, with 188 bones, its head in pristine condition, and over 11-inch-long teeth. It has often been used as the model for T. rex figurines and depictions. Casts of Stan sit in institutions such as the National Museum of Natural History in Washington DC and the National Museum of Natural Science in Tokyo, among many others, making it the most widely exhibited dinosaur of all time.

The skeleton, which stands 13 feet (4m) high and 40 feet (12m) long, including the tail, went up for auction at Christie's in New York on October 6, 2020. With an estimated sale price of around $8 million, Stan was expected to become one of the most expensive dinosaurs ever sold. Stan defied all predictions and sold for a whopping $31.9m, the highest price ever achieved by a fossil. At the time of writing, Stan's new owner remains anonymous, so where in the world the skeleton will end up is unknown.

2-Big Sue: $13.5M

It was huge news in the paleontology world when a 67-million-year-old Tyrannosaurus rex dinosaur was discovered in 1990 on the Cheyenne River Indian reservation in South Dakota. The specimen was discovered by paleontologists Peter Larson and Sue Hendrickson, and so the dinosaur was nicknamed Sue. To this day, though, it's still not known whether the dinosaur was male or female.

Sue is the largest and most complete Tyrannosaurus rex ever to be discovered. It was sold by Sotheby's in 1997 to the Field Museum of Natural History in Chicago, with funding help from Disney, McDonald's, and other companies and individuals. In exchange for their financial assistance, both companies got life-size casts of Sue; Disney installed its replica at Walt Disney World's Animal Kingdom. McDonald's, which received two casts, loaned them to museums and sent them on tour as traveling exhibits.

Her body is 42 feet (12.8m) long and has an estimated weight of at least 6.4 tons. She has become something of a celebrity in the dinosaur world and even has her own Twitter account @SUEtheTrex, which has almost 70,000 followers.

3-Prince, Apollonia and Twinky: $8M

A trio of Diplodocid Sauropod dinosaurs was found between 2007 and 2010 in a quarry in the small US town of Ten Sleep. It was a very rare find as the skeletons were more than 80% complete, with two of the skulls intact. They were nicknamed Prince, Apollonia and Twinky and were thought to be part of a herd or even family. Apollonia and Prince were adults and measured in at 78 feet (24m) and 89 feet (27m) from head to tail, while the baby dinosaur Twinky was 39 feet (12m) long. The National University of Singapore bought the trio from Dinosauria International, the Wyoming-based fossil company that found them, to display in the Lee Kong Chian Natural History Museum.

4-Dueling dinosaurs: $6M

This pair of dinosaurs locked in combat is among the most important dinosaur finds ever discovered. They were first found in June 2006, when rancher and amateur paleontologist Clayton Phipps was digging in Hell Creek, Montana, and came across what looked like a dinosaur pelvis. Returning to the site a month later to excavate, he discovered it wasn't just a pelvis but an entire skeleton – and it wasn't just one dinosaur, but two. After three months of extensive excavation, Phipps and his partners were able to determine the nature of their find: one of the most unique and best-preserved fossil specimens ever uncovered. The 67-million-year-old specimen includes both a juvenile T. rex and a Triceratops, buried together in the midst of what could be a deadly predatory encounter. Due to the nature of their burial, the skeletons are perfectly preserved in their natural positions. The Dueling Dinosaurs are still locked inside their ancient rock prison, bones partially concealed.

Bonhams tried to sell the dinosaurs back in 2013, after receiving a valuation by appraisers of $9 million. Getting the bones from Montana to the auction in New York was no mean feat: custom crates had to be used for each section, and a specialized truck with an air-ride suspension was used. The bidding lasted just 81 seconds and the highest bid, at $5.5 million, failed to meet the $6 million reserve.

The North Carolina Museum of Natural Sciences announced in November 2020 that it had acquired the "Dueling Dinosaurs" fossil. As yet, the dinosaurs have no names, unlike Dippy, Oskar or Stan in museums around the world.

5-The fighting pair: $2.75M

A most unusual discovery was made by paleontologist Henry Galiano in a quarry in Wyoming in 2007: a fossilized pair of dinosaurs locked in a predator-prey battle. The fighting dinosaurs turned out to be an Allosaurus and a Stegosaurus, with the Allosaurus' jaw wrapped around the leg of the Stegosaurus.

6-The mystery dinosaur: $2.35M

A 150-million-year-old dinosaur discovered in Wyoming went under the hammer at Aguttes auction house in Paris in June 2018. The fossil measured 8.5 feet (2.6m) tall and is 28.5 feet (8.7m) long and was reported to be in good condition, with about 70% of the skeleton intact. But this is a dinosaur with a difference. Paleontologists have been unable to identify what kind of dinosaur it is, only describing it as a carnivorous theropod. Experts say that the fossil resembles an Allosaurus, a dinosaur that reigned supreme during the late Jurassic period. However, several differences, such as the shape of the pelvis, skull, and teeth, indicate that it could be a dinosaur genus that scientists have never seen before.

7-The 'trophy' dinosaurs: $1.6M each

In April 2018, the Paris auction house Hôtel Drouot had a very good day when it sold two dinosaurs to the same bidder, a millionaire foreign collector. The specimens were a Diplodocus, measuring 39 feet (12m) long from nose to tail, and an Allosaurus, much smaller at 12.5 feet (3.8m) in length. Both roamed the Earth around 150 million years ago during the late Jurassic period.

8-The Triceratops from South Dakota: $657,250

This creature is a Triceratops and was found in Harding County, South Dakota, back in 2004. The skeleton measures a massive 19 feet (5.8m) long from head to tail, 11 feet (3.4m) across, and a towering 12 feet (3.7m) tall. The skull, which generally represents around 30% of a dinosaur's entire skeleton, was remarkably intact and only required a few minor restorations. Most Triceratops found in museums are made up of multiple dinosaurs, expertly put together to appear as one dinosaur. However, this piece is all from one dinosaur and was found 75% complete, making it very valuable. The huge dinosaur was auctioned off at Heritage Auctions in June 2011. Triceratops is the official state fossil of South Dakota.

9-Misty the dinosaur: $518,670

In 2009, German paleontologist Raimund Albersdörfer was excavating a quarry in Ten Sleep, Wyoming, when he told his sons to go off and explore so he could get on with some work. Sons Benjamin and Jacob returned sometime later and told their dad they had found a bone so big they couldn't carry it. The bone turned out to be a giant and very rare Diplodocus skeleton, nicknamed Misty after the "Mystery Quarry" it had been found in. Successfully removed, the bones were mounted on a frame in the Netherlands and then shipped off to England. Misty now stands at 14 feet (4m) high and 65 feet (16.5m) in length and is thought to be the first large dinosaur skeleton to be auctioned in Britain. Misty headlined at Summers Place Auctions in the UK in November 2013.

10-Triceratops skull: $242,000

This mammoth Triceratops skull measures an impressive 5.5 feet (1.7m) in length from the beak to the frill, making it one of the largest of its kind.

And at 80% complete, it is one of the most intact skulls ever found. Amazing when you think it had been buried for 65 million years. Triceratops was a rhinoceros-like dinosaur known for its large head. It could reach about 30 feet (9m) in length and 10 feet (3m) in height, making it one of the largest of all land animals. The skull was found on a private ranch in Montana and then tucked away in the rancher's house for years, preserved in field jackets and wrapped in plaster. The skull was sold at Bonhams Natural History auction in New York in 2009.

10.1-Freya the Harpocrasaurus: $123,000

A Harpocrasaurus is a duck-billed dinosaur that lived 75 to 67 million years ago and is almost as big as a Tyrannosaurus rex. This particular specimen, measuring around 25 feet (7.5m) long and 10 feet (3m) high, is virtually complete. Discovered in Montana in the 1990s, "Freya" was put on display at the Emmen Museum in the Netherlands, where she was given her nickname.

RUGS

Carpets have been a form of international currency since Marco Polo introduced the first rugs he brought from "the Orient" to the Italian aristocracy at the end of the 13th century. This is how the term "oriental rugs" came to be known to describe these treasures. The Persian Safavid dynasty that ruled from 1501–1736, a period now referred to as "The Golden Age of Persian Weaving," thanks to royal-sponsored workshops, produced many of the finest carpets the world has ever seen. When they surface, the most precious complete rugs in this category are usually purchased by museums. The collectible range is centered around best-of-the-best caliber rugs woven during the "Second Golden Age of Persian Weaving" (roughly circa 1800 to 1910). Included in this elite category are spectacular rugs primarily from Persia and the Caucasus Mountains, along with Turkey, India, and the Central Asian plateau.

Regardless of the region where they were made, investment-level rugs are created as entirely individual artistic expressions. Whether they were produced in city workshops, as part of the cottage industry of the smaller towns and villages or in isolated nomadic encampments, they represent the consummate achievement of only the most dexterous and sensitive weavers. They usually are virtuoso adaptations of the traditional designs, color palette and structure characteristic of that particular region.

Hand-woven silk-on-silk Persian or Oriental carpets are among the finest and most expensive in the world. Silk-on-silk rugs are hand-woven with super fine silk thread on a silk foundation instead of the less refined weaves such as silk-on-wool, wool-on-wool, or wool-on-cotton. All Persian rugs are made entirely by hand, from the shearing of the sheep to the weaving of the rug. This means that it takes much longer to produce each piece, and also, because it is handmade, every piece tends to be unique and different from any other piece. Even if the variation is very subtle, the difference will always be there because it was made by hand.

Collectors in Asia and the Middle East are investing in Persian rugs with the same enthusiasm as for rare, valuable contemporary works. Museums in the Middle East are also investing in Islamic art collections, including the Museum of Islamic Art in Doha and the Guggenheim Abu Dhabi. Renewed interest in Islamic art in the West has probably contributed to prices, too, with the 2011 opening of the Metropolitan Museum of Art's New Galleries for the Art of the Arab Lands and last year's opening of the Department of Islamic Art at the Louvre. Connoisseur-level buyers seek out the finest rugs in virtually every country of the world, so trading the best antique rugs is tantamount to trading fine paintings or other works of art.

Value metrics:

Core: Scarcity, Rarity, Provenance, Condition, Historical importance

Unique: Quality, Size, Artistry

Scarcity: Over the past two to three decades, fine rugs have seen their value appreciate due to greater demand. This situation is compounded partly by an embargo against Iran during the 1980s and 1990s, and partly by actions by the Iranian government to control the supply by passing a law limiting the number of carpets exported out of the country each year.

Rarity: A carpet with unique motifs and coloring tends to increase in value. Rare finds are carpets attributed to a famous master known to have produced very few pieces, an unusual location with a unique artistic style, or a specific era where few items have survived.

Provenance: Proving that the rug was indeed handmade by a known master is a key element in assigning value. The individual stamp of the particular weaver or weavers should be abundantly present. Illustrious ownership and being used at notable places add value.

Condition: This refers to the rug's general state; the material needs to feel soft and pliable. Cracking produced when folding a corner of the rug shows that the rug is very old. Age by itself does not matter. In fact, the older the rug, the higher the value, provided it is well-maintained and undamaged.

Historical importance: If the rug was a gift in honor of a special occasion or a visit to a historical personality, a rug owned by a famous ruler or representing a beginning or a turning point in regional style all constitute historically significant points raising the value of the rug.

Quality: The materials must be of the finest quality, both the silk or wool in the pile and the knots, as this will determine how well the carpet will age with time and use. The better the quality of the wool or silk, the longer the rug will last. The wool must be lustrous, luminous and soft, feeling like an alive material. Knot density, or knots per square inch, is important, because it objectively measures the complexity and tightness of how a rug has been woven. The more densely bound a rug is, the higher its quality and thus its price. The count should be no less than 100 knots per inch for a geometric design and 300 knots per inch for a floral design.

Size: Larger sizes are generally preferable and command larger premiums, as they require a lot more work, dedication and effort to produce, and also make a more powerful statement.

Artistry: The most important aspect is also the most intangible. To be considered investment-level, an antique rug must possess a stirring magnitude of artistry, a level of beauty that is literally breathtaking. Rugs that feature a vibrant palette of colors created from pure, natural dyes and unique patterns covering the entire rug make better investments.

Top 10 highest priced items:

1- Clark Sickle-Leaf Carpet - $33.74M

This extraordinary kaleidoscopic tapestry of leafy vines was woven in Southeast Iran in the early 17th century, measuring 9' by 6'6", and purchased by the Museum of Islamic Art in Doha.

2- Kirman Vase Rug - $9.6M

It's a blue leaf-patterned 11'1"x 5' 17th-century carpet from southeast Iran. Most Persian carpets are subdued in patterns and hues. This one is said to be the epitome of the "vase" technique, perfected during the Safavid dynasty in Persia. It's the first known rug to feature the popular Persian design called the Herati pattern.

3-Mughal Millefleurs "Star Lattice" - $7.7M

This Mughal carpet from India is owned by the Vanderbilt family.

4-Louis XV Savonnerie carpet - $5.7M

This 1750 carpet is one of three designed by Pierre-Josse Perrot and owned by Karl Lagerfeld.

5-The Pearl Carpet of Baroda - $5.5M

This 1685 masterwork of silk and fine deer hide with approximately 2,500 table-cut and occasional rose-cut diamonds set in silver, as well as foil-backed rubies, emeralds, and sapphires, all set in gold. It was originally meant to lie in the Tomb of Mohammad in Medina, Saudi Arabia. However, it never reached its original destination after the Maharaja of Baroda authorized its creation.

6-17th century Persian - $4.45M

This silk 17th century 7'7"x5'7" Isfahan rug is an exceptional example of Safavid art during the reign of Shah Abbas (1587–1629). Some of the factors contributing to the price are exceptionally high knot density, use of 14 different hues, outstanding craftsmanship, and the use of pure silk. Despite its age, the rug was in very good condition with negligible end loss at the time of the sale.

7-Louis XV Savonnerie carpet - $4.4M

Three carpets of this exact design by Pierre-Josse Perrot were made for the Crown Furniture Repository in France, the administration responsible for furniture and art inside the royal residences. This carpet, woven sometime between 1740 and 1750, was the last one produced.

8-Safavid 16th century rug - $4.3M

This silk, wool, and metal-thread prayer rug is inscribed with Persian verses in nastaliq. The inscriptions suggest that it may have been a diplomatic gift from the Safavid Persian court to the Ottoman Turks.

9-Tabriz Medallion Carpet - $2.4M

This 16th century 20' long carpet was stolen from the Rothschild family in Austria by the Nazis during World War II. Its purchaser was the Sheikh al-Thani of Qatar.

10-Safra rug - $2M

This 16th century East Persian 27'4"x11'3" Safavid rug is part of the Safra family's collection.

FURNITURE

The antique furniture market has been in protracted decline for decades. The most recognized expert and author in the space, John Andrews, decided to end his annual audit of the trade in 2017, after publishing the Antique Furniture Index since 1968. The 2016 final issue showed the index down to a level last seen in the 1980s. While there's no single reason for the market decline, there are two easy culprits to help explain it. The first reason is the simplest: Taste has changed. The second is demographic change, where many people who could afford to buy $100,000 dining tables in the 1970s, '80s, and '90s are dying. Their heirs are less than eager to hold on to their parents' furniture or acquire similar pieces. As they look to unload, the rising stock and diminished demand are causing prices to slump and will likely continue to do so for years to come.

Antiques that are durable, small and easily transported have a tremendous edge over ponderous, fragile furniture, china and other unwieldy collectibles that grandma may have favored. Over-sized massive furniture housed in a castle may sell to a museum, but may not be attractive to many individuals who want an antique for a house built in the last fifty years. The logistics of owning large, heavy pieces can be a barrier for an investor. Just moving them can be very costly, and the structure supporting them may require reinforcement. There are exceptions to the trend. Although the overall market for antiques is shrinking, activity at the very top remains strong, as ultra-wealthy buyers acquire the finest museum-grade pieces, regardless of category, period or origin. Rare pieces and those with exceptional provenance or high quality can still garner high prices. Unique, high-end vintage furniture pieces have "boosted" furniture design to the same status as fine art. Many fine-art-priced furniture pieces are purchased by museums or collectors who pay a high premium for original items in mint condition. Interest in certain types of vintage furniture is rising, and sales of so-called mid-century modern furniture from the 1950s and 60s are especially strong.

Specialty antique furniture has the power to defy expectations when pieces with the right provenance catch buyers' imagination. As recently as November 2017, Bonhams sold an exceptionally rare set of four 16th century Chinese huanghuali folding chairs to an Asian buyer for $6.9M. A rare pair of huanghuali tapering cabinets from the Ming dynasty from the same collection sold for $2.2M.

Value metrics:

Core: Scarcity, Rarity, Provenance, Condition, Historical importance

Scarcity: As even the best furniture is not made to last for centuries, or to be immune from ongoing damage from regular use, it is not unexpected that over decades and centuries, a lot of pieces were lost, irreparably damaged or just had their condition reduced far below mint. Given this natural attrition of items, as well as the difficulty of preserving the remaining ones in top shape, investment-grade items are very scarce and will continue to be even more so going forward.

Rarity: Historically, before mass production, each piece was one of a kind, and for the high-end items, usually only one or at most a few copies were produced. If we consider that wars, changes of tastes, regular wear and tear, and age have impacted even some of the remaining examples, it will be apparent that locating these in good condition is difficult. Thus, the rarity factor adds a great deal of value.

Provenance: If a piece belonged to a well-known historical figure, be it royalty, art or a music heavyweight, or if it was located in a famous location such as a palace, then this metric can play a major part in value determination. As with all other collectibles, traceability of ownership from creation to the present day is of paramount importance.

Condition: Only the most immaculately preserved pieces, in mint condition or as close to it as feasible, tend to command high premiums. If a piece includes highly unusual or precious materials or textures, this is also part of its condition and is reflected in the value.

Historical importance: This can carry additional weight, such as the first models of a new decorative style or an integral part of a major historical event. This metric is not a significant extra contributor to value, as most valuable pieces are primarily such because of the scarcity and rarity element.

Top 10 highest priced items:

1-The Badminton Chest - $36.7M

The most expensive piece of furniture ever sold, this cabinet features amethyst quartz, apart from other precious stones. The masterpiece was created by thirty designers, and the process took them six years. The antique was made in Florence and is believed to have been belonged to the third Duke of Beaufort and was sold off by his descendants in 2004. The cabinet can currently be found at the Liechtenstein Museum.

2-The Dragons Chair - $27.8M

Designed by Irish designer Eileen Gray, The Dragon's Chair was created between 1917 to 1919. When it was placed for auction, the estimated price of the chair was 2.3 million. An ardent admirer of it chose to bid ten times that amount of it, which is the reason for its high price tag. The furniture has been handcrafted from leather and carved wood. The proud owner of this timeless chair was Yves St Laurent.

3-Antique Secretary Desk - $11.4M

This Goddard and Townsend desk was made during the 1760s. Only nine examples of this antique secretary desk were ever made, making it a rare and expensive piece of furniture.

4-Huanghuali folding chairs - $6.9M

Of all furniture remains from the Ming dynasty (1368-1644), the folding horseshoe-back armchair is the rarest. Their complex construction and fragile design made them subject to greater wear and more susceptible to damage. Made from exotic woods and sometimes from carved lacquer, with decorative metalwork strengthening the joints and hinges, these horseshoe-back folding chairs were used by the imperial family, persons of rank and scholars. Fewer than 30 of these horseshoe-back armchairs dating to the Ming dynasty when the design reached its pinnacle are known to exist.

5-The Harrington Commode - $5.9M

Though not a very glamorous household item, a commode was once used by wealthy families. It served not only as a useful item but also as a piece of furniture that was aesthetically beautiful. The Harrington Commode was created by the renowned craftsman Thomas Chippendale in the 18th century.

6-The Tufft Table - $4.6M

Carved by hand in 1700, The Tufft Table was named after its creator Thomas Tufft. It narrows at the end and features a range of details and decorations. Custom made for Richard Edwards of Lumberton, New Jersey, this ROCOCO-style table has pierced fretwork along with a detailed ball and claw feet.

7- Isamu Noguchi Table- $4.5M

Made at the request of A. Conger Goodyear, President of the Museum of Modern Art, Noguchi designed his first table for the living room of Goodyear's weekend house in Old Westbury, New York. Comprised of stack-laminated rosewood and Herculite plate glass, the Goodyear Table mimicked the building's texture and materials for which it was commissioned, the Goodyear House by Edward Durrell Stone.

8-George II Parcel Gilt Padauk Cabinet - $3.9M

This intricate piece of craftsmanship was sold at Christie's in 2008. It was created by the well-known designer Thomas Chippendale, who also designed the Harrington commode (#5 on the list), which is one of the main reasons for its high price tag.

9-Huanghuali tapering cabinets - $2.2M

These rare objects of the Ming dynasty are from the same collection as the Huanghuali folding chairs. Chinese furniture is generally made without any glue or nails. The pieces are held together by a complicated network of joints instead.

10. Ruijssenaars Magnetic Floating Bed - $1.6M

Ruijssenaars Magnetic Floating Bed is truly an incredible and innovative piece of furniture. Architect Janjaap Ruijssenaar collaborated with Bakker Magnetics to create this piece of furniture. It took the makers 6 years to build the bed, which uses repulsive magnetic forces to levitate it. It can float 40 cm above the floor, withstanding a load of up to 900 kilograms.

MUSICAL INSTRUMENTS

Music is a form of art, which derives from the Greek word meaning "art of the Muses," ancient Greek goddesses who inspired the arts, such as literature, music, and poetry. Music has been performed since the dawn of human time with instruments and through vocal songs. Instruments were objects created solely to make musical sounds. The oldest object that some scholars refer to as a musical instrument is a simple flute, made from animal bones and dates back as far as 37,000 years. However, most historians believe that determining a specific time of musical instrument invention is impossible. Many early musical instruments were made from animal skins, bone, wood and other non-durable materials.

Piano

The piano is an acoustic stringed instrument invented around 1700, most likely by Bartolomeo Cristofori of Padua, Italy. Its predecessor was the harpsichord. It is played by using fingers on a keyboard, causing hammers within the piano body to strike the strings. The Italian word *piano* is a shortened form of the Italian word *pianoforte,* which means "soft" and "loud."

Most pianos are of mediocre quality, even if they have great sentimental value. A century ago, every home aspired to have a piano. Now, there is a massive glut of these old pianos, even though demand has gone. A sought-after piano with a good name and quality build is still a recession-proof investment, as families tend not to skimp on education, and pianos can be a big part of this.

Steinway is by far the most respected and recognized brand. Still, there are numerous other great makers, including the 'three Bs' of Blüthner, Bechstein and Bösendorfer, as well as the early Steinway family offshoot Grotrian-Steinweg, plus the modern piano-maker Fazioli, that also attract investors who want a quality name but do not want to buy new.

The investment market focuses on second-hand pieces. A Steinway grand typically start at about $20,000 depending on the condition and the model, whereas a 50-year-old Steinway commands, on average, a price that is more than nine times its original price tag. A Steinway Model D-274 built in 1900 sold for around $1,400 would fetch around $100,000 today. Steinway might be best known for its grand pianos, but a Steinway vertical or upright piano can also command a handsome resale value as well, selling, on average, at twice its original price.

Grand pianos are the most collectible because they are the rarest and tend to offer superior acoustics. Over the past decade, the most collectible grand pianos prices have doubled, thanks to an increase in demand from international musicians, particularly those in China.

Value metrics:

Core: Scarcity, Rarity, Provenance, Condition, Historical importance

Scarcity: A combination of instrument age and piano type makes for a scarce instrument. Top makers like Steinway are able to make only a limited number of instruments due to its very labor-intensive and expert-driven process. From this small starting set, pianos get damaged with age, so there is a natural attrition rate, creating a smaller population of available ones each year.

Rarity: Unique features or decorations making the instrument one of a kind or one of a small set, combined with the model type, create the rarity factor for pianos.

Provenance: Much like all musical instruments, the famous musicians who played it, international awards won with it, and ownership by important musical or historical figures make for a desirable object.

Condition: The piano needs to have been regularly tuned, maintained, and ideally continuously played over time to ensure it remains near the original condition.

Historical importance: The importance of a piece can be enhanced by being the first of its kind to be created, the first or best created by a famous maker, or simply by being used by a famous composer or musician during key periods of their career.

Top 10 highest priced items:

1-Crystal Piano, Heintzman-$3.22M

This piano earned its name since every inch of it is made from real crystal. The piano was designed and constructed by the piano company Heintzman. It has been seen and played in front of a billion spectators at the 2008 Beijing Olympic Games. The piano was then retired after its one and only performance, but it has been said that it was a performance of a lifetime.

2-John Lennon's Steinway Model Z - $2.37M

This is a Steinway & Sons creation that belonged to John Lennon and the very instrument on which his famous song, "Imagine," was written.

3-Red Parlor Grand Piano, Steinway & Sons - $1.925M

Bono, the lead singer of the band U2, wanted a two-toned masterpiece that would take center stage at the Red Auction to be held in New York for a charity to help fight AIDS, Tuberculosis and Malaria in Africa.

4-Sound of Harmony Concert Grand, Steinway & Sons - $1.63M

This Steinway was custom designed and built for a Chinese art collector named Guo Qingxiang. Forty layers of wood were used to construct it, which gives it an incredible acoustic-type quality. It took 3 years to design and build, and Steinway signed his name using crystallized gold instead of ink like his other pianos.

5-Galaxy Piano-$1.36M

This very futuristic piano is one of only five ever created. It was designed for those who have a strong eye for detail, such as a 24-carat gold plated body of fiberglass, automatic lid and curved keys.

6-The Kuhn Bosendorfer Grand Piano-$1.2M

The infamous glass sculptor John Kuhn, and piano maker L. Bosendorfer Klaviefabrik, collaborated to create this remarkable diamond and jewel piano. It features about 100,000 jewels that were individually polished by hand-cut glasses. The 7'4" black piano is actually so shiny that it looks like a gem itself. The two wanted to make sure the piano really appealed to women, so they included diamond patterns of gold leaves surrounding a crystal on the top of the piano.

7-Alma-Tadema Steinway-$1.2M

This was constructed in 1887 by Sir Lawrence Alma Tadema, a name that is not familiar to most people. One hundred years later, Steinway and Sons made an exact replica of the original piano that exhibits arched brass lyre, intricately hand-carved case, legs and lid, along with mother of pearl inlaid pieces.

8-Marilyn Monroe's Baby Grand Piano - $662,500

Marilyn's mother, Gladys, originally owned the piano, but it wound up in someone else's hands when it was sold after her passing. Marilyn tracked it down, and it was a treasured possession of Marilyn's for years, until she, too, passed on at a very early age.

9-The Casablanca Piano, Richardson's Inc. - $602,500

One of the most notable pieces from the timeless movie is the piano featured in one of the most iconic scenes, "As Time Goes By," right alongside Humphrey Bogart and Ingrid Bergman. Back in the day, the piano was considered one of the grandest, with its now faded yellow-green finish.

10-La Mort du Cygne, Erard- $409,000

The La Mort du Cygne, Erard (The Dying Swan), was custom built out of Mahogany wood in 1906 by some of the most renowned French artists of that time. It was designed using striking golden-brown and tans for the color palette and is one of the most elegant pianos ever made.

Violin

Violins are likely to have been developed from a number of other string instruments of the 15th and 16th centuries, including the vielle, rebec, and lira da braccio. The instrument's overall pattern was set in the 17th century by luthiers like Antonio Stradivari, the prolific Amati family, Jakob Stainer of the Tyrol, and many makers at the time and since followed their templates. The earliest evidence for their existence is in paintings by Gaudenzio Ferrari from the 1530s, though those instruments only had three strings. The Academie musicale, a treatise written in 1556 by Philibert Jambe de Fer, clarifies the violin family much as we know it today.

Instruments benefit from being a stable market, with notable demand over supply between collectors and players. Though historically not widely recognized as assets for investment, rare stringed instruments are gaining interest due to the continual increase in value, growing demand and finite supply. The restricted supply and increasing demands from international markets accelerate the gains for rare and fine instruments. With greater than 150 years of valuation, studies have demonstrated that fine classical Italian instruments have historically increased at approximately 3-5% per annum. Over the past 20 years, many instruments in the top tier have climbed in value 12-25%.

Restricted supply and increasing demand from markets such as Russia, China and Korea have increased the value of rare and fine instruments. Large institutional buyers have not only created more competition, but have placed pressure on the rare stringed instrument market by reducing the number of instruments on the open market. This undeniably accounts for the continued increase in prices on the international scene and escalated demand. Research conducted by Nobuyoshi Ozawa at the University of Cincinnati estimated the market capitalization for rare stringed instruments (those made over 150 years ago by the top 270 makers) to be approximately $12.3 billion. 100% of this market turns over every 30 years, making it a surprisingly liquid market.

Value metrics:

Core: Scarcity, Rarity, Provenance, Condition, Historical Importance

Unique: Age, Maker

Scarcity: The restricted supply and increased demands from international markets accelerate the gains for rare and fine instruments. This trend has been augmented by an increasing number of musicians from emerging markets determined to make their mark on the world stage backed by super-rich collectors who share their patriotic sentiment, with Asian players being the most prominent new factor.

Rarity: There is a finite supply and limited access to these rare examples of the violin family, with approximately 600 Stradivari instruments and 140 Guarneri del Gesu violins known to have survived till today. A diminishing supply due to the ravages of war, natural disasters and accidents throughout time has inspired institutions to collect and preserve the rarest examples.

Provenance: Documents such as provenance, certificates of authenticity, condition reports are an important part of the process and help provide reassurance in an investment. Technology has even entered the buying process, but it does come with additional costs. Reports such as dendrochronology reports and CT scans further help identify an instrument and review it for hidden damage.

Placing an instrument with the right musician has benefits beyond philanthropy. Having a musician perform on an instrument not only maintains its tonal brilliance, but also helps to elevate the prestige of the instrument. Also, a history of prominent recordings and concerts is more desirable to a future buyer. The Duport Stradivarius Cello, named after its one-time owner, 19th-century cellist Jean-Louis Duport, the 1711 Stradivari-crafted cello was purchased by the Nippon Music Foundation in 2008 for $20 million. Its high value is partially due to its visible dent, rumored to be caused by Napoleon Bonaparte's boots when Duport allowed Bonaparte to handle the infamous cello, proving that superb provenance trumps condition.

Condition: A significant consideration in valuation: an item with extensive restoration or needs restoration doesn't offer as much investment value as a more pristine specimen. Often an item that has had some wear from use identifies it as an item that works well for working musicians. This raises the possibility that the reduced condition may be coupled with a stellar provenance of being used by one or multiple celebrities, counteracting or trumping the condition factor.

Historical importance: The importance of a piece can be enhanced by being the first of its kind to be created, the first or best created by a famous maker, or simply by being used by a famous composer or musician during key periods of their career.

Age: Instruments have the distinct advantage of appreciating in value with age. Their tone grows in depth as their unique story adds to the resonating qualities of the instrument. The main difference between a $1,000 and a $10,000,000 violin is the tone. Many violins that sell for over $1,000,000 are at least 100 years old, which means their wood has had time to age in such a way that they sing. Violins made in Cremona, Italy, during the city's golden age of violin making, around 1650 to 1750, are the most highly regarded violins among players and collectors.

Maker: Even if one does not know about violins, most people have heard the name Antonio Stradivari, who is universally celebrated as one of, if not "the" finest violin maker throughout history. An innovator in his time, with exquisite craftsmanship and artistry, Stradivari had a prolific career. His instruments are noted for their tone and quality of materials and continue to inspire violin makers today. Stradivari is not alone in this premier class of making some of the finest violins from the golden age of violin making in Italy during the 17th-18th century. Guarneri del Gesu, Giovani Battista Guadagnini, Nicolo Amati, Domenico Montagnana and recently Bergonzi are among the makers whose work can range in price from $1,000,000 – $15,000,000.

Top 10 highest priced items:

1-The Messiah Stradivarius - $20M

Crafted in 1716 by Antonio Stradivari, a world-renowned maker of the best violins in the world during his golden period, it stayed in his shop until his death in 1737. Violinists do not play it as much, hence its relatively new condition.

2-The Vieuxtemps Guarneri - $16M

Crafted by violin maker Guiseppe Guarneri del Gesu in 1741, the instrument got its name from Henri Vieuxtemps, a Belgian violinist who once owned it. Other violinists also had the chance to use this violin are Itzhak Perlman, Yehudi Menuhin, and Pinchas Zukerman.

3-The 'Lady Blunt' Stradivarius –$13M

Made in 1721 by Antonio Stradivari, during his 'Golden Age,' 'The Lady Blunt' has passed from collector to collector, ensuring that it has remained in almost original condition. It has hardly been played and so was not subject to the alterations seen in most 18th century violins.

4-The 'Molitor' Stradivarius – $3.6M

It belonged to Juliette Récamier, a socialite and prominent figure of the First Empire immortalized in several paintings, most famously by Jacques-Louis David. In 1804 the violin was passed on to Gabriel Molitor, a general of the Empire and a musician, and remained in his family until the First World War.

5-The 'Hammer' Stradivarius – $3.54M

This violin, designed in 1709 during Antonio Stradivari's '*Golden Age,*' is named after the Swedish collector Christian Hammer. It was previously owned by the Nippon Music Foundation, which loaned it to violinist Kyoko Takezawa.

6-The 'Solomon, ex-Lambert' Stradivarius - $2.4M

This 'late' 1729 Stradivarius does not date from the famous maker's '*Golden Age*' but rather from his later '*Mature*' period. The violin gets its name from two of its owners, the British violinist Dorothy Mary Murray Lambert, a pupil of Carl Flesch and Leopold Auer, who had a career as a soloist in the 1920s and '30s, and the American entrepreneur and co-founder of *Vanguard Records*, Seymour Solomon.

7-The 'Baron von der Leyen' Stradivarius – $2.35M

Antoni Stradivari's masterpiece dates from 1705, the '*Golden Age*' of the Italian luthier. It takes its name from an early owner Baron Friedrich Heinrich von Freidrich von der Leyen, a wealthy German textile merchant who appears to have had a keen interest in instruments.

8-The 'Folinari' Guarnerius Del Gesu – $2.3M

Made by Giuseppe Antonio Guarneri, known as Guarnerius de Gesu (of Jesus) in Cremona in around 1725.

9-The 'Lady Tennant-Lafont' Stradivarius – $1.7M

Made in 1699 by Antonio Stradivari, the instrument first belonged to violinist Charles Philippe Lafont, a pupil of Rodolphe Kreutzer and a contemporary of Niccolo Paganini. It was bought by a wealthy Scottish businessman, Sir Charles Tennant, in 1990 for his wife Marguerite, an amateur violinist.

10-The 'Red' or 'Mendelssohn' Stradivarius – $1.7M

Created in 1720, it was called '*The Red Violin*' because of its vivid red hue. After being played for a time by Joseph Joachim, it then seems to have disappeared for nearly 200 years before resurfacing in Berlin in the 1930s with Lili von Mendelssohn (a descendant of Felix Mendelssohn).

TOYS

An action figure is a poseable character doll made most commonly of plastic and often based upon characters from a film, comic book, military, video game or TV show. In 1971, Mego began licensing and making American Marvel and DC comic book superhero figures, which had highly successful sales and are still considered highly collectible today. The 1980s spawned many popular action figure lines based on cartoon series such as Masters of the Universe, G.I. Joe, Thundercats, The Real Ghostbusters and Super Powers Collection. These were some of the most successful marketing tools for toy companies. As the '80s were ending, more and more collectors started to surface, buying up the toys to keep in their original packaging for display purposes and future collectability. This led to the flooding of the action figure toy market. One of the most popular action figure lines of the late '80s and early '90s, Teenage Mutant Ninja Turtles action figures were produced in such high quantities that the value for most of these would never be higher than a few dollars.

The toy market has taken off over the past couple of decades, and vintage toys can make a fortune at an auction. Childhood favorites evoke sentimental feelings, which make them highly collectible. When enough people with money are nostalgically drawn toward a particular thing, it becomes valuable. Typically, about two decades after a toy is popular, the kids who played with it have become adults with a yearning to recapture their youth. They want their childhood back, and one way to do that is to buy a piece of it. This is known as the "20-year rule." Toys based on or inspired by popular TV shows or movies, such as 'Star Wars,' are usually more valuable. Unboxed LEGO sets can also sell very well, along with unique board games, model trains, early American cast iron money banks, quality dolls and teddy bears.

A sub-category of collectible toys are mechanically complex examples from the 19th century, such as transportation-related toys, including trains and cars, and early European tin toys that are handmade and hand-painted. Any antique toy in the original box has added value, sometimes because the box itself has great pictures on it.

Value Metrics:

Core: Scarcity, Rarity, Condition

Unique: Events

Scarcity: Items related to popular video games, TV shows and movies that are not produced by the millions are relatively scarce. For example, limited-edition LEGO sets (unassembled), Original Minecraft and Fortnite toys, and limited-edition board games (Monopoly) all fall into that category. The most valuable toys are the ones that were only produced in small quantities for a very limited period of time.

Rarity: Adds value but collectors quickly abandon impossible-to-find toys. The Star Trek 1701 collection, where only 1,701 iterations of each figure were made, famously angered fans and damaged the Star Trek line. Most toys were meant to be played with, therefore finding vintage pieces unboxed and in mint condition can be difficult, also contributing to the rarity factor. The cardboard typically got thrown away, so boxed items are much rarer.

Condition: For a toy to be worth the most, it must be in excellent condition, unopened, in the box, and have its original packaging. The box's value is more than just the nostalgia of seeing the box for the first time; an unopened box is a guarantee of a toy's pristine condition. Nothing is in mint condition if a kid has played with it, but it can be in excellent condition. For instance, when it comes to old Star Wars figures, for a Luke Skywalker to be worth $1,000 or more, it has to come in the original bubble wrap package.

Many important factors contribute to a figure's grade and value, including the backing card, completeness (with accessories), and being free of dents, scratches and marks. One of the most important ones in determining an action figure's grade or value is the backing card's condition. Most collectors are looking for MOC or MIB (Mint On Card / Mint In Box) figures, which are presumed to be in a Mint or Near Mint condition as they have never been taken out of their original packaging. If the card is damaged and in poor condition, particularly on older or rarer figures, the toy's value decreases considerably.

The two main grading companies are AFA (Action Figure Authority) and CAS (Collector Archive Services). A figure bearing an AFA grade will often sell for 2-3 times more than the equivalent ungraded figure, with AFA Gold graded figures known to fetch as much as 10 times the price of ungraded figures on eBay. Both AFA and CAS grade on a scale of 1-100, with 10 being very poor and 100 being Gem Mint. The AFA Grading Scale consists of Gold, Silver and Bronze levels, where Gold is the Premium level covering grades 100, 95, and 90; Silver grades 85, 80, and 75, and bronze 70 and below. Once graded, each action figure is sealed in a hard acrylic storage case to preserve its graded condition. If the figure is at any time removed from its case, then the grading becomes null and void. Professional grading also includes separate autograph verification services, as is already the case with comic books and trading cards. Having a photo with the star of the movie while getting the action figure signed increases the value. If signed at a professionally organized convention, a certificate of authenticity (COA) will be included. Over the last few years, there has been a significant increase in the number and variety of action figures available from movies, sports, pop groups/bands, and TV. This has resulted in an increased demand to have the action figures autographed by the star or character depicted by the action figure.

Events: If a toy goes viral on social media, there is a good chance that the toy will soon jump in value. If a new movie or cartoon with the characters has just been released, it will also impact the desirability and thus price, albeit temporarily.

Top 10 highest priced items:

1-G.I. Joe a Real American Hero - $200,000

1963 prototype G.I. Joe. Handmade by series creator Don Levine

2-Rocket Firing Boba Fett - $185,500

This 1979 Boba Fett figure was equipped to fire rockets from his backpack. Kenner swapped the firing rocket for a glued-on part after a child allegedly swallowed a projectile. After it was deemed a choking hazard before its release, it never made it to stores. But a few of the prototypes still float around, including an unfinished blueish grey one

3-Vlix - $45,430

Vlix came from a short-lived animated series in 1980 called Star Wars: Droids. While there was a first wave of figures released, the second wave (which Vlix was a part of) was scrapped when the show was canceled.

4-Darth Vader - $30,000

In 1978, when Star Wars action figures were first hitting the market, the Luke, Obi-Wan and Darth Vader figures all came equipped with a cunning telescopic light-saber accessory. Clever though it was, the mechanism was fragile and the effect unconvincing, so manufacturer Kenner hastily redesigned the figures, and a collectors' item was born.

5-Elastic Batman - $15,000

This Batman figure was produced by a toy company called Mego, along with stretch versions of characters like Donald Duck, Mickey Mouse, and Casper. Only two Batmans are known to have survived.

6-Babe Ruth McFarlane - $13,600

Only five of these unique Ruth's with the blue hat were made (instead of traditional white Yankees hat). Two are in McFarlane Toys' archives; three were released to the public hidden among shipments of regular Ruth's.

7-El Capitan Rayo $8,000

Somehow, a South American toy company called Gulliver acquired the mold for Superman and released their own hero in Columbia. They just used different colors and painted The Flash's symbol on his chest.

8-G.I. Joe Nurse $6,000

The figure flopped due in part to toy stores that didn't know whether to put her with the war toys or the Barbies.

9-Batman Robot: $5,000

This figure was produced by a Japanese company called Nomura in 1966 and was unavailable in the U.S.

10-Computron: $5,000

From the world of Transformers, Computron was the name given to the massive combination of the Technobots when they joined to form one robot (Scattershot, Strafe, Lightspeed, Afterburner, and Nosecone). One could have purchased Computron as part of Hasbro's 1986 collection, but it was only available as a gift set.

VIDEO GAMES

A rapidly emerging collectible area is old video games, the new kid on the block when it comes to collectibles. As the third-party grading of vintage and even modern-era video games has become a valid business, demand for video game-based collectibles is soaring. Still, collectors should use extreme caution before spending large sums of money on these unproven collectibles. Expert grading plays such a crucial role, with VGA and Wata being the two most recognized ones. Many of the same speculators who helped drive up the prices of graded vintage comic books over the years, with the advent of CGC, Comics Guaranty Corporation (the first well-respected third-party grading company of comic books), now enter the vintage video game marketplace en masse.

As the video game collecting industry grew during the late 2000s, hobbyists gravitated toward the games with which they grew up. Those were also some of the first console games on the market in video gaming's short history. When third-party grading services entered the hobby, collectors finally had an objective measure of one game's value vs. another's. This is similar to the system that had been in place for years in baseball card and comic book collecting.

Value comes from two places in video game collecting. Firstly, games become valuable when they are, in fact, great games. The quality of the player's experience can heavily dictate its value as the game ages. Also, the older the game is, the less pristine it is expected to be, and therefore, when someone has a cartridge with no signs of wear or tear, it sells well. For hardcore collectors, a physical copy reigns supreme. Digital copies could disappear or get deleted, leading to someone losing their beloved title. Thus, physical copies are the only mark of true ownership in the eyes of hardcore collectors.

Increasingly, there is a movement away from collecting based on nostalgia and toward a view of games as rare collectibles. In years past, the hobby was dominated by aging gamers. Today the interest is mainly from the same sort of serious collectors who consider coins, baseball cards, comic books and works of art as an integral part of their investment portfolios.

Value Metrics:

Core: Scarcity, Rarity, Condition

Unique: Events

Scarcity: This translates to sealed copies of video games made in relatively small amounts for the first run for a specific geography or a narrow test market (like the first release of Super Mario Bros only in New York and Los Angeles in 1985). Only 2,000 to 10,000 copies of each of the 27 test market games were ever made, and only a few dozen exist in sticker-sealed style across the whole test market line.

Rarity: For games, the packaging type increases rarity, like in the original Mario Brothers NES games that came with a foil sticker instead of being sealed in shrink-wrap. Items like this usually exhibit significant wear after more than 30 years, making well preserved and pristine examples that much rarer.

Condition: There are two leading video game companies: VGA (Video Game Authority), part of the Collectible Grading Authority line of companies including AFA, and WATA Games. While VGA does grade items that WATA Games does not (items like actual video game systems and accessories), WATA Games is the market leader for graded vintage video games at the present time.

VGA and WATA Games use two entirely different grading scales when grading games: VGA uses the modified toy grading scale of 10 through 100 that goes up in 5-to-10-point increments. WATA Games uses the comic book 1 through 10 grading scale, with decimal-based levels. This is causing confusion on the secondary market for collectors who pursue both VGA and WATA graded games. For example, a WATA Games 9.0 is a very fine/near mint (VF/NM) game. A VGA 85 graded game is a near mint plus (NM+) graded video game, which is actually several grades higher.

Events: Various promotional events designed to commemorate the anniversary of important dates such as a specific game release generate a spike in interest for older games. As a result, demand is significantly increased for a period of time before the anniversary.

Top 10 highest priced items:

1. 1985 NES Super Mario Bros - $150,000

Perhaps the most iconic of all video games, this Wata Games 9.8 rated near-perfect specimen with an A+ seal rating is the highest priced game to date, although that is likely to be changing. A copy of a cartridge sealed with a small round sticker with the Nintendo logo in a "near mint" grade of 9.4 and an A++ seal rating from Wata Games was sold for over $115,000, while a lower-quality 8.0 rated copy of the same game sold for over $40,000.

2. Nintendo World Championships (Gold Cartridge) - $100,000

Nintendo organized a global video game tournament called the Nintendo World Championships and manufactured custom NES cartridges for the game. While 90 copies were made in the standard gray, an additional 26 were colored gold and were given away as prizes in a Nintendo Power contest. The gold cartridge is the rarest NES cartridge in existence and sold for $100,088 on eBay in February 2014.

3. Stadium Events - $41,300

This was a game released in 1987 by Bandai. Nintendo wound up buying the rights to the game in 1988 and pulled all the copies of the original *Stadium Events* from the store shelves. They were supposed to be destroyed. However, about 200 copies had already been sold, and of those, about 20 complete copies are said to still be out there somewhere. To have a full-intact box for the game is very rare, and boxes alone can sell for up to $10,000 by themselves.

4. Air Raid - $33,433

This game was put out by Atari in 1982 and is a shoot 'em up game, meant for the Atari 2600, and designed by Men-A-Vision, which are said to have only developed the one game. It's estimated that only 12 copies were created, and the authentic ones can be distinguished by an odd light blue color cartridge and a T-shaped handle. This copy is the only truly complete version, with the cartridge, instruction manual, and the box that has been publically sold.

5. Superman - $30,000

The standard release of Superman on the Atari 2600 is extremely common. However, a rare version with Superman' and 'Sears Tele-Games' written in yellow letters and only sold in Sears stores was produced in far fewer numbers. This pristine example was a sealed, unopened and boxed copy.

6. Nintendo Campus Challenge - $20,000

Nintendo holds frequent competitions on college campuses. The *World Championships* version gave players six minutes to play for the highest score on games like *Dr. Mario, PinBot, and Super Mario Bros. 3*. When the tour ended, most of the copies of the games were destroyed, with only a few surviving.

7. 1990 Nintendo World Champions (Gold and Gray Editions) – $20,000

The first Nintendo competition was held in 1990 and toured twenty-nine cities throughout the U.S. The competition was named for the game cartridge released in the same year, and the gold and gray editions of the original cartridge are some of the most expensive video games ever sold.

8. Tetris Mega Drive - $17,000

Sega believed it held the rights to publish a home console version of Tetris when in reality only Nintendo did. As a result, it was forced to pull its version of Tetris and destroy all copies of the game right before it went on sale. Still, a tiny number of copies – no more than 10 – weren't destroyed and exist to this day.

9. Red Sea Crossing – $13,877

In 1983, programmer Steve Schustack created Red Sea Crossing, an Atari 2600 game about Moses crossing the Red Sea. The game wasn't promoted in games magazines; instead, it was aimed at religious publications. For a while, Red Sea Crossing was believed to be a hoax that didn't actually exist because nobody had seen a copy, even though Schustack was sure at least 100 were manufactured. At the time of writing, only two copies of Red Sea Crossing have ever been seen.

10. Kizuna Encounter - $12,000

Sometimes a game is only rare in certain regions. Nowhere is that better demonstrated than with Kizuna Encounter, a fighting game released for the Neo-Geo, which was a rare system with less than a million sold worldwide. The vast majority of those console sales were in Japan and the US, but a few were made for the European market using the PAL format. It's believed that only 12 copies exist, but only five have ever been seen.

10.1 Nintendo Powerfest 1994 – $10,988

Nintendo only produced about 33 cartridges of this game. They were used in stores all across the country to be a part of about 130 different events, with the winners of each of the events going to the World Championships. At the end of all the events, all of the cartridges were returned to Nintendo except one, which eventually ended up in the hands of a game collector who paid for this rare one-of-a-kind game cartridge.**Grading agencies (toys and video games)**

Rating agencies	Toys	Video games
AFA (Action Figure Authority)	x	
CAS (Collector Archive Services)	x	
VGA (Video Games Authority)		x
WATA Games		x

Grade ranges	Toys	Video games
AFA (Action Figure Authority)	1-100	
CAS (Collector Archive Services)	1-100	
VGA (Video Games Authority)		1-100
WATA Games		1-10

Desired grades	Toys	Video games
AFA (Action Figure Authority)	80-100	
CAS (Collector Archive Services)	80-100	
VGA (Video Games Authority)		80-100
WATA Games		9-10

TRADING CARDS

Sports

Soccer

As the most popular sport globally, with an estimated 3.5 billion fans worldwide, soccer is an emerging market for collectible cards. From Pele to Lionel Messi, almost every player will have a couple of expensive options, but some are worth far more than others.

Despite a couple of vintage options, it's clear that more recent cards are some of the most valuable overall. That's likely due to the time it took for collectible soccer cards to become more popular worldwide, compared to more US-centric sports such as basketball or baseball. Soccer cards are still very underpriced, thus creating a good profit potential, even when looking at cards of the best players in the history of the sport.

Top 10 highest priced items:

1-1958 Pele Alifabolaget Soccer RC #635 - $288,000 ($315,000 via Rally Rd)

Brazilian-born Edson Arantes do Nascimento is widely regarded as the single greatest player in the history of the world's most popular sport. Like many of history's most celebrated figures, so famous is the undisputed king of The Beautiful Game that he is known throughout the world by one name: Pelé. When organizations around the globe began naming their "century" awards in 1999, the International Olympic Committee elected him its Athlete of the Century. The Fédération Internationale de Football Association, or FIFA, the governing body of soccer, named him a joint winner of its Player of the Century Award. However, the Brazilian forward was unknown when this rookie card was released, as it was issued during the 1958 World Cup in Sweden.

While Pelé appeared on several additional issues in 1958, the Alifabolaget card has spearheaded the recent international revival in soccer cards. PSA NM 7 specimen recently sold for more than $43,000 in an online auction, and PSA's listing of auction results cites the sale of a PSA NM-MT 8 copy for $100,000. This is a PSA 9 graded card, one of just five examples at its tier (with none graded higher) among a total of more than fifty copies recorded in PSA's census reporting (only 2 years ago in 2018, this card sold for just $57,000 in a 2018 Heritage auction).

2-2004 Lionel Messi Panini Mega Cracks RC #71 - $116,000

The current GOAT (Greatest of All Time) of the soccer world, Lionel Messi, will be long remembered for his incredible talents. The star player for possibly the best club team that the world has ever seen, he failed to replicate those heights with Argentina.

This card is unquestionably the most important modern soccer rookie card in existence. Only twenty have managed to earn the elite assessment largely due to limited production and condition sensitivity. Often plagued by a slew of issues, this PSA 10 specimen is virtually uncirculated and is free of typical edge imperfections with incredibly clean and pristine surfaces. The few intelligent collectors who are lucky enough to own one of these twenty are reluctant to sell as it's widely speculated that this could very well be a $250,000+ card in the very near future.

The 2004 Panini Mega Cracks is a great option, seen as Messi's definitive RC. It has a strong action shot of the player dribbling in his famous Barca colors, with the ball stuck to his feet. With his retirement looming in the next decade, now could be the perfect time to get on the Messi hype train before prices rise even further.

3-2002 Christiano Ronaldo Panini Sports Mega Craques RC #137 - $41,211

The first card to make the list features a shot of a teenage Ronaldo with the ball at his feet while wearing the green and white stripes of Sporting. The 2002-03 Panini Sports Mega Craques is widely seen as his true RC, and this PSA 10 Gem Mint option is priced accordingly.

4-2002 Cristiano Ronaldo Panini Futebol Stickers RC #306 - $25,000

Stickers aren't always the most popular option with collectors, especially if there's a card from the same year available. When it comes to Ronaldo, it's okay to make an exception for his 2002-03 Panini Futebol Stickers release PSA 10 version. It features a strong profile shot of the Portugal skipper as he lines up for his club team, with enough gel in his hair to identify it as an early '00s sticker. Mint editions are comparable in value to the Panini Craques.

5-1991 Zinedine Zidane Panini Foot '92 RC #43: $22,000

Zinedine Zidane is a maverick former Real Madrid and France captain, possibly best known for head-butting Italian midfielder Marco Materazzi in a World Cup final. He's now the head coach at La Real, leading the team to a trio of Champions League victories. The dynamic midfielder played in the 1998, 2002 and 2006 World Cups for France, and scored five goals. Zidane helped the host team win the 1998 World Cup, defeating Brazil in the final game.

Zidane's '91 RC is one of the more important cards from the decade. This PSA 8 graded copy is one of the highest-rated examples on the market. It features Zidane's image with a full head of hair, scowling at the camera in his Cannes kit. The card has a solid yellow border, making it more difficult to find in higher grades due to chipping.

6-1958 Pele Monty Gum International Footballers RC - $16,768

The second Pele card to make the list is also considered to be an RC. Featuring a dated illustration of the Brazilian superstar, it has the appearance of a playing card on the front. Pele is the Ace of Spades, showing how quickly his reputation grew after the '58 World Cup. He's also featured on the 4 of Clubs, which has a red back. Just two of the known examples have earned the PSA 7 grade, with only one grading higher.

7-2018 Kylian Mbappe National Treasures RC Soccer #39 - $11,300

Kylian Mbappe is seen as the next big thing in football, exploding onto the scene with Monaco in the Champions League in 2016-17. He was snapped up by PSG for a rumored €145 million-plus €35 million in add-ons, making him the highest-paid teenager at the time.

The Bronze Parallel PSA 10 card focuses on a feature-length image of Mbappe in his international kit against a white and red background. The numbered parallels are the most valuable overall, especially the platinum (/1) and /5) emerald versions, with the serial number at the front of the card.

8-2019 Cristiano Ronaldo Panini Chronicles #CR7 - $10,100

2019 Contenders Historic Ticket Autographs subset features the legendary Cristiano Ronaldo in a classic Manchester United kit. A stickered autograph at the bottom makes this PSA 10 example of 1 of 23 Cracked Ice parallels version a rare and highly desirable investment.

9-1995 Ronaldo Panini Voetbal 95 RC #80 - $8,000

Before Cristiano Ronaldo made headlines, Ronaldo Luís Nazário de Lima was the Ronaldo everyone talked about. The prolific scorer finished with 15 goals in his World Cup career, including appearances in 1998, 2002 and 2006. Ronaldo was also on the 1994 World Cup Champion roster, but did not play. He currently sits as the top overall scorer in World Cup history.

Ronaldo led Brazil to the title in 2002 and second place in 1998. Despite his relevance to the game and the fact that he is a modern player, there is not a large supply of Ronaldo cards available.

His PSA 10 Panini Voetbal 95 has a shiny border and a unique cut, which is always going to make it more expensive than the norm. It's a great investment piece, and it's likely to be coveted by anyone lucky enough to see him play at his peak.

10-2003 Cristiano Ronaldo Upper Deck Manchester United #13,14,15 - $7,000

As he's most strongly associated with his time with Manchester United, it's no surprise to find one of his first cards being popular with fans of the best-supported club in the world.

There are three different base cards to mark his inaugural season in England, flitting between the red, white, and black kits they used that season. There are also a couple of signed parallels in the same set, with a base red card numbered to 39 and a black parallel that features a different image and is numbered to 25, the relative rarity making this PSA 10 card additionally desirable.

10.1-2010 Lionel Messi Panini World Cup South Africa Premium #44: $4,000

The second Messi card on the list is from the 2010 World Cup. As it's newer than the RC, it's way more affordable, despite a stunning design. The chrome background of this 1 of 23 version is shaped like South Africa, which was hosting the World Cup that year, and Messi is pictured in his Argentina kit. The PSA 10 version of this card last sold for $4,000 + in 2020.

Boxing

Boxing isn't baseball in terms of popularity, but then nothing is like baseball in terms of trading cards. Still, basketball is giving it a run for the money. The problem with boxing cards is that not only is the sport not baseball, but it's also not even close to any of the other American sports leaders. In terms of relevance and popularity, it is woefully behind not only the heavy hitters like baseball, basketball, and football, hockey, but even less popular spectator sports like golf and tennis.

As a result, while collecting sports cards is very popular, boxing cards have been a far less desirable area for collectors. Even though many of the cards are not plentiful, if not too many people care about them, the value isn't ultimately going to be very high.

Top 10 highest priced items:

1-1960 Hemmets Journal Boxing Cassius Clay Muhammad Ali ROOKIE RC: $90,000

This PSA 9 near-pristine card is easily one of the most important rookie cards in existence. It is seldom seen on the market in grades higher than PSA 8, with PSA 8.5 selling for $27,500 and another PSA 9 for $50,000. It possesses beautifully cut edges with virtually perfect centering, a rare and desired combination of attributes. This is a vastly undervalued rookie card of one of the most important figures in the sports world.

2-1946 Leaf Rocky Graziano: $87,330

This PSA 6.5 graded card is the ultimate boxing collector's card. Very few companies have produced boxing cards, and the Leaf Brands' 1948 set of 49 all-time greats is one of the best. For years collectors thought that the Leaf gum company's "Knockout" set consisted of 49 cards, erratically numbered. The 50th card was supposed to be Graziano, but he refused to sign off on it because of what was believed to be a contract dispute. Nevertheless, a handful of cards made it into circulation. They are now as rare as the T206 Honus Wagner, but not yet quite as valuable.

Uncut sheets of the cards could be found that were exactly 7 cards by 7 cards, but about 10 years ago, a Rocky Graziano Leaf emerged, and since then, one more has been found. A recent auction saw a lower graded PSA 5 Graziano Leaf card sell for over $40,000.

3-1888 SF Hess & Co. N332 Set - $80,000

This set is believed to contain more than 80 cards. However, these blank-backed cards are extremely hard to come by and therefore command big dollars whenever they hit the market, and they don't surface that often. As proof of these cards' rarity, a recent sale saw a card in very poor condition, with fading and heavy creases sell for well over $100, with PSA 5 graded cards selling at around $1,000.

4-1910 T226 Red Sun Jack Johnson SGC 80 EX/NM 6: $19,120

Graded SGC 80 EX/NM 6 by SGC, this is a 1-of-1 with none graded higher treasure. In fact, this is the only example graded to date by the top two grading services. Johnson became the World Heavyweight Champion by defeating Tommy Burns in Australia on December 26, 1908, becoming the first black man to accomplish that feat.

5-1910 E125 American Caramel Jim Jeffries - $19,120

Strong and durable, Jeffries style was to fight in a crouch position, with his formidable left arm extended. With an 18-1-2 record (14 by KO), Jeffries retired undefeated in 1904, but returned to the ring on July 4, 1910, to fight heavyweight champion Jack Johnson, a fight he lost in the 15th round.

6-1985 Panini Supersport Italian Mike Tyson RC DNA AUTO #153: $15,000

Along with Ali, Tyson is arguably the most coveted and revered figure in boxing. This PSA 8 graded example of the rookie card of one of the greatest modern boxers came from a sticker set from Italy where most were stuck to a sticker album, and very few survived with the back on them. The card is regarded highly among investors and yet remains woefully undervalued compared to demand.

7-1951 Topps Ringside Rocky Marciano #32: $14,400

This PSA 9 graded card is one of just three recorded in MINT, with none rated higher. Rocky Marciano is a true boxing legend and the Heavyweight division's only undefeated champion.

8-1951 Topps Bob Murphy Ringside #49: $12,000

Due to the card's rarity, specimens with high grades, like this PSA 8 graded card, command high premiums. Although not a high-profile boxer, this short-run card is very hard to come by, and as in the Adventure sets, many Topps Ringside sets sold do not have card number 49 included. This card generally commands hundreds of dollars in good condition (a recent eBay auction for a PSA 6 Ex-MT card sold for $1,026), and cards in fair to average condition can still fetch hundreds of dollars.

9-1886 N167 Old Judge Jem Smith, Horizontal Reverse - $8,950

Graded 30 GD 2 by SGC, this is the ONLY example of this card known in the hobby. English Heavyweight Champion Jem Smith fought both bare-knuckle (his preferred method) and with gloves. His battles were so raucous at times that the police had to intercede on several occasions.

10-John L Sullivan 1889 Spaulding & Merrick N386: $6,500

From a series of 24 subjects of mostly actors and actresses, the number 7 card is the heavyweight champion, John L. Sullivan. Sullivan's legacy is without equal. A titan of the ring, the Irish giant brawler fought not only trained men, but would perform exhibitions where a $500 bounty was offered to any man brave enough to oppose him. This is an SGC 50 Ex 5 graded example.

10.1-Max Schmeling 1956 Gum Products Inc. Adventure Card #86: $1,000

The Adventure series featured boxers in front of their national colors. This card is a very rare card featuring Max in front of the Nazi symbol of the Swastika. This card was taken out early in the set's release due to its offensive nature. These cards were sold in vending machines, very similar to the old single vend stamp machines. You put a nickel in, pushed the slide in, and got a folded cardboard insert with the card in it. These cards are generally in good shape when found because they usually hadn't been removed from the cardboard. Most Adventure Gum sets for sale on the market come without this card.

Golf

PGA Golf trading cards have had a rocky and up-and-down history. These cards do not have the same value as the big sports cards like football and especially baseball cards, but still hold some value with dedicated collectors.

The history of golf trading cards is sporadic, especially early on. Golf cards were first introduced in 1901 by Ogden, and there were some golf cards produced in the early 1900s, while Goudey had a couple of golf cards mixed in with other sports stars in their Sport Kings set in 1933. After this, there were pretty much no golf cards produced until about 35 years ago.

The first company that produced a full, mass-produced set of cards was Donruss in 1981 and 1982. These are the first golf cards that most modern era collectors recognize, so the Donruss golf cards are considered rookie cards for many of golf's biggest stars, like Nicklaus, Kite, and Watson, though they actually made their debuts years earlier.

Over the next 20 years, PGA Golf trading cards were issued on and off. The two companies that issued most of these cards were Grand Slam Ventures and Pro Set. For the most part, these sporadic issuings of cards did not sell well at all.

The first-time collectors recognized a set of golf trading cards as being "popular" was in 2001. This was when Upper Deck released their first golf cards. The obvious reason for this line's sales success is that it contained the Tiger Woods "rookie" card. This is probably the most expensive of the modern golf trading cards, selling for hundreds of dollars depending on the variety and print run. Woods was also included in an earlier set of cards in 1987. This set was issued by Grand Slam Ventures, but because it wasn't really issued to the masses, some don't consider it a real trading card. Others believe it's Tiger's true rookie card, since it dates from his PGA Tour debut.

While Upper Deck's line was popular at first, they stopped making the cards in 2005. They still have a deal with Tiger to distribute signed memorabilia. Since this time, there has not been a complete set of golf cards mass-produced. Upper Deck announced in late 2020 that it would launch three golf releases in the spring of 2021, including the Artifacts brand that's been used in numerous Upper Deck sports card products over the years. The 2021 golf edition is described as a "premium product" that will be heavy on memorabilia and autograph cards from both current PGA and LPGA stars and former players.

Top 10 highest priced items:

1-1996 Tiger Wood Sports Illustrated Card: $125,000

In 2001, a gem mint (PSA 10) version of this card, which was in a perforated insert with seven others in the December 1996 issue of Sports Illustrated for Kids, sold in a private sale brokered by Mike Souza for $125,000. Since then, Woods' popularity has had ups and downs, and the card has been heavily counterfeited. Today, a card in this condition will go for around $10,000-$15,000. There have been plenty of PSA 8s and 9s that are available for less than $1,000.

2-1932 Bobby Jones U.S. Caramel: $80,000

This extremely rare high-grade PSA 9 example is a key card featuring golf's first true superstar. After finding his groove and winning the 1923 U.S. Open, Jones never looked back, winning 13 Majors in only 20 attempts. He only trails Jack Nicklaus and Tiger Woods in that category. In 1930, Jones would become the only man to ever win golf's version of the Grand Slam (U.S. and British Opens as well as U.S. and British Amateurs). Furthermore, Jones didn't just win; he embarrassed his competition. During a 36-hole playoff in the 1929 U.S. Open, Jones beat Al Espinosa by 23 strokes. In 1974, Jones was inducted into the World Golf Hall of Fame.

3-1998 Champions of Golf Masters Collection Tiger Woods ROOKIE RC: $64,000

This PSA 10 graded card is one of only two confirmed examples in the world and is simply impossible to locate in such a high grade. To date, PSA has graded 8,481 examples, with only two ever being awarded the illustrious GEM MINT designation.

4-1973 Panini Jack Nicklaus Rookie Card: $40,000

This PSA 10 graded card is 1 of 4 to achieve this status. Jack Nicklaus was a star from the moment he beat Arnold Palmer in 1962 till the end of his career in 1986, when he retired with a record of 18 Major Tournament wins.

5-2001 SP Authentic Golf Gold Tiger Woods ROOKIE RC AUTO /100: $35,000

This PSA 10 graded card is the other official rookie card for Tiger Woods, with one of the top-selling Tiger Woods autographs out there. Even with a print run of 900 copies, prices remain strong. The simple and modern SPA Authentic Stars design utilizes an on-card autograph to make one of the most popular Tiger Woods cards ever issued. The gold parallel (#/100) adds to its rarity.

6-1933 Bobby Jones Goudey Sport Kings: $30,000

This is the single most important golf card in existence and a key to the extremely popular 1933 Goudey Sport Kings set. Considered by some to be the greatest golfer of all time, Jones is the only golfer to make an appearance on the list of the top 5 most expensive golf cards more than once. His first entry is from the same Goudey Sport Kings set as the famous Walter Hagen card. Simple in design, but boldly presented, the PSA 9 graded Jones card is 1 of only 2 in existence.

7-1932 Gene Sarazen U.S. Caramel: $28,800

The legendary Sarazen helped create the modern sand wedge and is best remembered for his famous "shot heard round the world" at the 1935 Masters Tournament. The thin-stocked U.S. Caramel set features many baseball players and boxers and only two golfers: Sarazen and Bobby Jones. Condition sensitive and appealing to set collectors and golf fans alike, this is the only known PSA 9 graded example of the card.

8- 2001 SP Authentic Golf Tiger Woods ROOKIE RC AUTO /900 #45: $21,300

This BGS 9.5 graded example is the most desired rookie card of the legendary golfer and comes within a pristine quality autograph.

9-1926 Lambert & Butler Bobby Jones ROOKIE RC #2: $15,000

This PSA 9 graded card of one of the legendary Co-founders of the Master's Tournament and founder and designer of the Augusta National Golf Club is a true rarity. Jones remains the only golfer to ever win the "Grand Slam," which he accomplished in 1930 by winning all four of the sport's major tournaments. He is equally as famous for retiring from competition after realizing this unprecedented and still unmatched achievement.

10-1933 Walter Hagen Goudey Sport Kings: $9,825

One of the greatest golfers of all time, Hagen still occupies third place for most majors in a career behind only two first-name legends: Tiger and Jack. Hagen has a huge following, and this makes his card especially desirable.

The Goudey Sport Kings set is another multi-sport set and is widely collected by baseball card collectors, too. The thicker stock makes the Goudeys easier to find in strong condition. Still, PSA 8 and above are very rare, and this PSA 8.5 graded specimen is the highest known.

10.1-1965 Arnold Palmer Bancroft Tiddlers Giants of Sport: $3,500

Most collectors consider this PSA 8 graded card Arnold Palmer's true rookie card. A PSA NM 7 sold for $1,500 in 2010.

All cards:

Value Metrics:

Core: Scarcity, Rarity, Condition

Scarcity: Most of the more desirable top cards were initially printed in small amounts, and as most of them are quite old, the amount of any type of these cards on the market is very limited, much more so for those in decent condition. Many diehard fans place a lot of emotional value on their prized possessions. This combination of small volumes and few willing sellers at any price creates a high scarcity condition.

Rarity: Many top cards are either one of a kind, a key part of an important set, or are one of the few existing that were not taken out of circulation for various reasons. Most of these highly sought-after examples are rarely, if ever, on the market, exacerbating the original scarcity to a new level.

Condition: The most in-demand cards are the graded examples with high grades. Both PSA and BGS provided grading services for game trading cards. For more modern cards, the value lies in the PSA and BGS 9 to 10 graded cards. With older ones that are much harder to find preserved in good condition, PSA 5 and higher is considered an excellent grade.

Table 2

Trading cards summary:

Assets	Soccer	Boxing	Golf	TOTAL
1	$288,000	$90,000	$125,000	**$503,000**
2	$116,000	$87,330	$80,000	**$283,330**
3	$41,000	$80,000	$64,000	**$185,000**
4	$25,000	$19,000	$40,000	**$84,000**
5	$22,000	$19,000	$35,000	**$76,000**
6	$16,750	$15,000	$30,000	**$61,750**
7	$11,300	$14,400	$28,800	**$54,500**
8	$10,100	$12,000	$21,300	**$43,400**
9	$8,000	$8,950	$15,000	**$31,950**
10	$7,000	$6,500	$9,825	**$23,325**
TOTAL	**$526,300**	**$352,180**	**$448,925**	**$1,346,255**

The good news for fans of soccer, boxing and golf, is that an amazing world-class collection of top-of-the-line items can be put together for less than the cost of just one high-priced basketball card.

Gaming

Yu-Gi-Oh

Yu-Gi-Oh! is a Japanese manga series written and illustrated by Kazuki Takahashi about a boy named Yugi Mutou, who solves the ancient Millennium Puzzle. It was serialized in Shueisha's Weekly Shōnen Jump magazine between September 30, 1996, and March 8, 2004. Two anime adaptations were produced; one by Toei Animation, which aired from April 4, 1998, to October 10, 1998. Another was produced by NAS and animated by Studio Gallop titled Yu-Gi-Oh! Duel Monsters, which aired between April 2000 and September 2004. The manga series has spawned a media franchise that includes multiple spin-off manga and anime series, numerous video games, and a trading card game known as Duel Monsters that lets players use cards to "duel" each other in a mock battle of fantasy "monsters." In North America, Magic has an overall larger player base, but worldwide it still goes to Yu-Gi-Oh! with the largest player base in Japan and Korea. As of 2018, Yu-Gi-Oh is one of the highest-grossing media franchises of all time with over $30B in revenues.

Value Metrics:

Core: Scarcity, Rarity, Condition

Scarcity: Most of the top cards were initially printed in extremely small amounts, and because they were awarded as prizes, the number of cards on the market is very limited. Die-hard players place too much of an emotional value on their awards to easily part with them. This combination of small volumes and few willing sellers creates a high scarcity condition.

Rarity: Some of the cards that are either one of a kind or part of a very small set are predictably very rare. Being unique or one of very few is a precondition for rarity. Most of these are rarely, if ever on the market, exacerbating the original scarcity to a new level. The ultra-rare one-of-one cards, much like iconic MTG cards such as the 1996 World Champion or Shichifukujin Dragon, are especially prized and sought after.

Condition: The most in-demand cards are the graded examples with very high grades. Both PSA and BGS provided grading services for game trading cards, and the value lies in the PSA and BGS 9 to 10 graded cards. Grading companies give a sense of security for less knowledgeable investors who want to avoid counterfeits, and provide value to the truly dedicated collectors, who want to have the most flawless piece of anything they collect.

Top 10 highest priced items:

1-Tournament Black Luster Soldier - $2M

One-of-a-kind card printed on stainless steel was the prize of the first-ever Yu-Gi-Oh! tournament in 1999.

2-Blue-Eyes Ultimate Dragon - $400,000

One of a kind prize for a winner of the 2001 Asian Championship Series, that came with a signboard that has a signature from Kazuki Takahashi, the original creator of Yu-Gi-Oh!

3-Dark Magician Girl - $50,000

Only 100 examples of this card were awarded as prizes in a Japan-exclusive lottery.

4-Amatsu-Okami of the Divine Peaks - $18,800

A few were given out to the top players (not champions) of all three categories of the 2018 Yu-Gi-Oh! World Championships. So far, only one Amatsu-Okami of the Divine Peaks was put up for sale.

6-Iron Knight of Revolution - $12,999

Only three copies of the Iron Knight of Revolution were given out at the 2017 Yu-Gi-Oh! World Championship. Only one Iron Knight of Revolution was ever sold.

7-Armament of the Lethal Lords - $9,000

Given to the winners of the World Championship Series in 2006.

8-Skuna, The Leonine Rakan - $6,000

The prize at the Yu-Gi-Oh! World Championships in 2009 with only six cards known to exist.

9-Cyber-Stein - $3,000

Only 18 of the special Cyber Steins were awarded at the Shonen Jump Championship events from December 2004 to July 2005.

10-Minerva the Exalted Lightsworn - $2,300

Given as a prize at the 2015 Yu-Gi-Oh! World Championships.

Virtual game highlights

The sports card and memorabilia boom has come on the coattails of surging cryptocurrency markets that are constantly setting new all-time highs and investors looking for hard assets to hedge against future inflation. The newest and most cutting-edge entrant in this emerging space is NBA Top Shot started in July 2019 as a joint venture between the NBA, the NBA Players Association, and Dapper Labs. Their products are digital highlight videos of unique sports moments. The concept takes the relatively new fractional ownership model for collectibles to the next logical and technologically advanced step. Collectors have gotten very comfortable with the idea of effectively virtual ownership that comes from buying fractional shares of cards on sites like Collectable or Rally Rd without ever seeing the card.

The NBA owns all the highlight reels, but the collectors own the limited-edition numbered version, which they can collect, trade and sell. The NBA cuts the highlights, and Dapper then figures out how many of each they will sell and numbers them. They then put them into digital packs, just like traditional cards, and sell the packs for between $9 and $230, depending on the quality of the highlight, the player, and how limited it is. Upon purchase, those highlights go into a buyer's encrypted, secure highlight wallet.

Unlike cryptocurrencies which are completely fungible and readily exchangeable, each NBA Top Shot moment is a non-fungible ERC 721 token (NFT) used "to create verifiable digital scarcity." Digital ownership with each Limited-Edition collectible is marked at creation with a unique serial number and guaranteed by the blockchain. Anyone can view a particular highlight on YouTube, and those who own NBA Top Shot moments don't get any incremental revenue from views. However, the value of the virtual reel is in the scarcity that Dapper creates.

Just like in traditional card packs, collectors can get common cards or coveted highlights, with each moment's value determined by its scarcity and rarity. After packs sell out, the only way to acquire NBA Top Shots digital highlight reels is on the global, open, peer-to-peer, always-on marketplace. Buyers never know exactly what is in a pack until they are opened, and it is possible to also trade sealed packs on the marketplace. Every single transaction on the marketplace happens within seconds. Everything related to authenticity and payments is automatically taken care of by a blockchain called Flow. All transactions are immediate without waiting for a card to be graded, delivered, or authenticated.

When something sells on the marketplace, both Dapper and NBA get a cut, unlike a traditional trading card deal, where licensing rights are based on projected primary sales and never take into account the secondary market. Since its launch, the company has registered nearly $32 million in sales over nearly 500,000 transactions with close to $2 million in trading volume in January 2021 alone.

Value Metrics:

Core: Scarcity, Rarity

Scarcity: Every moment and every set belong to a specific series, which corresponds to milestones in the NBA year. Once a series ends, all sets in that series are closed and will remain complete forever. Certain players are more expensive to purchase than others as only the most performing players are likely to retain a fan base and value in the future. The demand for moments associated with them greatly exceeds the available supply.

Rarity: Each set is associated with 1 of 5 different collectible tiers: Common (1,000+), Rare (150-999), Legendary (25-99), Platinum (1/3) and Genesis (1/1), the rarer a moment, the higher the value. For a given moment in a set, the lower the serial number, the higher the value, sometimes by as much as 20x. If a moment's serial number matches the player's jersey number, there's an additional premium attached to the moment.

Top 10 highest priced items

1. LeBron James: $71,455
2. LeBron James: $47,500
3. Ja Morant: $43,313
4. Ja Morant: $35,000
5. Giannis Antetokounmpo: $34,999
6. LeBron James: $26,543
7. LeBron James: $25,000
8. Zion Williamson: $24,500
9. Giannis Antetokounmpo: $20,000
10. Luka Doncic: $19,000
11. Kawhi Leonard: $11,999

Collectibles summary:

Table 3

Metrics	Cigars	Vinyl	Gems	Jewelry	Guns	Gaming cards	Swords	Wooden decoys	Autographs	Count
Brand	x	x		x	x					4
Quality	x		x	x						3
Maker		x						x	x	3
Age	x						x			2
Rating	x	x								2
Events		x			x					2
Region			x							1
Size	x									1
Shape	x									1
Usability						x				1
Count	6	4	2	2	2	1	1	1	1	

As we can see from the table above, the key intrinsic value metrics that can be used to describe the key drivers of value for collectible assets remain the same for even more exotic collectible assets. All graded assets, where the condition is by far the most important driver, are not really concerned with provenance or historical significance, except in extremely rare instances.

CONCLUSION

This book illustrated a number of ways fractional participation in revenue streams generated by a wide variety of activities from poker to wine can be an option worth considering if ongoing and recurring income is an important component of your financial plan. The ability to supplement cash flow with proceeds from investments periodically without having to dispose of them to create liquidity can be valuable, especially when planning for future cash outlays. Being able to size your initial exposure to various verticals is a key benefit of the fractional approach. You can control your risk much more effectively than when having to commit to buying the entire asset. Additionally, each time you receive a part of your investment back, the total amount at risk for a given investment is reduced until, at some point, you get back over 100% of your original investment. Then you begin enjoying the stage of investment where you are playing entirely with "house money," i.e., with all future payments being pure profit.

The ideas discussed in this book require the desire and ability to thoroughly understand each of the revenue streams considered, as there are aspects that are not easily understood or commonly known. The analytical framework required to evaluate them closely resembles that used by early-stage venture capital firms when conducting due diligence on prospective start-up investments. It may initially seem overwhelming to create and implement consistently. If you want to grow your understanding of the right approach to thinking about this emerging opportunity, as well as get step-by-step instructions on how to develop your personal investment policy, you can take a course specifically designed to walk you through the approach, examples, and final investment decision making. It is available for early sign-up at https://michaelfoxrabinovitz/courses.

The various exotic assets described in the second half of the book have been selected because they are commonly known and understood, making them good candidates for future fractionalization. However, most are impractical to invest in at the present time, as they have not been actively included in the universe of investments core fractional platforms use. My first book on fractional investments, "Own A Fraction, Earn A Fortune," has been very well received by collectible enthusiasts and investors. Hopefully, it has helped thousands of people create and grow their wealth and build a more secure future for themselves and their families. If you want to learn about ways to incorporate fractional collectible investing into your financial plan, please check out my book at http://michaelfoxrabinovitz.com/ or find it directly on https://www.amazon.com/dp/B08QB9KRFX.

Author Biography

Michael is currently a partner with Chartwell Capital providing investment management services. He is planning to continue his role there as well as expand his involvement in providing investment advice and consulting services in the collectible investment field. He is an active investor in the collectible space across most of the major platforms.

Previously, he was a partner with Capricorn Partners, delivering a range of risk management, portfolio review and data analysis solutions to premier players in the financial industry.

Over the last 25 years, he held a variety of roles that allowed him to gain an appreciation of the art of investing from various angles: launching two hedge funds in alternative fixed income space, actively managing assets across multiple strategies, creating portfolio evaluation tools, implementing asset allocation and portfolio construction programs for many UHNW families, and serving as a trusted advisor to top US and global financial players.

Michael holds a B.S in Economics from Wharton School of Business and an MBA from Columbia University Business School. He is also a holder of Chartered Financial Analyst (CFA), Chartered Alternative Investment Analyst (CAIA) and Financial Risk Manager (FRM) designations.

Apart from his passion for collectibles, his hobbies include travel, poker, scuba diving, playing guitar, and writing poetry.

Acknowledgments

It is a pleasure for me to acknowledge the key people who have made this book possible.

First of all, I want to thank my parents, Michael and Marina, whose constant and unwavering support and encouragement made this book possible.

My debt of gratitude goes to my friend and long-time business partner Lev Grzhonko, who has been insisting that I write this book for many years, and I am glad that he finally persuaded me to do so.

Special thanks to my editor James Lee, an invaluable resource both as an amazing editor and a subject matter expert.

Made in the USA
Las Vegas, NV
26 September 2023

78178228R00075